How to Get the Family You've Always Wanted

How to Get the Family You've Always Wanted

Developing Healthy, Purposeful Families

Martin Sanders

CHRISTIAN PUBLICATIONS, INC.
CAMP HILL, PENNSYLVANIA

CHRISTIAN PUBLICATIONS, INC.
3825 Hartzdale Drive, Camp Hill, PA 17011
www.christianpublications.com

Faithful, biblical publishing since 1883

How to Get the Family You've Always Wanted
ISBN: 0-88965-234-1
© 2004 by Martin Sanders
All rights reserved
Printed in the United States of America

04 05 06 07 08   5 4 3 2 1

To Dianna, I agree with our kids:
You are an amazing mom.
Thanks for the memories.

To Bo and our daughter-in-law Christie,
and to Amie, Eric and Lauren,
you've made it all worthwhile.
You are loved more than you could know.

To Norm and Lois,
you modeled life and love and memories.
Thank you.

Contents

Preface

*H*ow to Get the Family You've Always Wanted is designed to give your family hope and to help you develop workable structures to implement in your day-to-day life. You can work together toward your dream, reach it, enjoy it and pass on the benefits to those around you and to generations to come.

The patterns of my own family serve as the framework for much of the content of this book, but so do the experiences of thousands of other families. The research didn't begin seventeen years ago in libraries but with interaction and interviews with individuals and their families. We talked about reflections, patterns, feelings, effectiveness and regrettable challenges they had experienced.

In my own family we did a great deal of experimenting. Dianna and I discovered that by the time our two older children were ten or twelve years old, we were not necessarily doing well by other people's standards. Most of what we were "supposed to do" did not work for us. We informed the children that we were going to use them as guinea pigs. We were aware it could work out really well, or it could be disastrous, but we were willing to take that risk. What seemed like subtle risks to us appeared quite significant to others.

We consistently used empowerment models with our children, giving more permission than most families would and little consideration to hairstyles, clothing and even curfews (unless serious abuse occurred). We focused more on lifelong and eternal issues of the heart and soul: how decisions are made and how people are treated, personal values and love. Sometimes the outcomes looked better than at other times, but now that all four of our children are in young adulthood, we really like the outcomes (as of this week!).

What Is Behind This Book

This book has come about in two ways: First, it's a compilation of my interactions with families; and second, it's a combination of two primary passions that have been part of my life in the past twenty years. The first great passion has been discipleship, mentoring and coaching as a developmental process. I've conducted my life as a reflective practitioner who focuses on how people develop and change personally, spiritually, professionally and particularly in areas of character formation. I have participated in church, work and conference settings with individuals and groups in more than thirty countries. The second great passion of my life has been the intentional development of families, both individuals within the family and the family as a unit, in multiple countries and cultural contexts.

My personal interview process began when I decided to interview first 100 and then another 100 college students when my own children were entering the teen years. I wanted to see patterns of effectiveness and patterns of futility, not from the parents' perspectives but from the eighteen- to twenty-one-year-olds' perspectives. Much of what I learned through those interviews affected my own parenting style, my observations about families and the informal way I interview people for research patterns and coach them about their own families and relationships.

Another factor that influenced this book was the weekend discipleship conferences I conducted in more than sixty churches ten to twelve years ago across Canada and the northwestern United States. One of the sessions of the seminar included a component on how to make intentional faith work in family structures. Out of those experiences came requests to do entire conferences on discipling families.

Ten years ago I began to offer a graduate course on Family Life Development at the institution where I teach. It is a culturally diverse institution close to New York City, so I've assisted students with research projects and have read hundreds of their studies, which represent more than thirty countries or cultural contexts. The differences and similarities within each cultural situation are intriguing indeed.

As founder and president of Global Leadership Inc., I've had the opportunity for more than a decade to see principles of family development lived out in some forty countries. The mission of Global Leadership is to develop and empower the next generation of Christian leaders for effective ministry around the world. We take groups of up to fifty leaders, ages twenty-five to forty, through a series of character-based leadership development experiences. The goal is that these young people, who have been recommended to us by their organizations, then reproduce this model in a small group of peers. In working with young leaders, it's also necessary to work with their families. Many of the frameworks and illustrations found in this book come directly from interactions with these young world leaders.

I do not work primarily with families in other countries; rather, I work with emerging young leaders who have families. As mentor and coach, my job is to help them effectively focus their life, mission,and goals. Doing that most efficiently and effectively often requires a focus on relationships—family relationships in particular. These very personal interactions with nearly 2,000 people in ten to twelve countries per year offer significant amounts of material for personal research and trend extrapolation.

Another avenue of gleaning observations for this book has been the development of a series of seminars conducted under three names: "Coaching Your Family," "Mentoring Your Family" and "Discipling Your Family." The titles and content are adjusted, depending on the audiences and desired outcomes. The series never was intended to become yet another content-driven seminar for churches; rather, the talks began because of requests primarily from Russians and Canadians whose church leaders had been significantly influenced by Global Leadership.

Finally, this book came about because leaders, communities and churches who had been influenced by earlier coaching or seminars asked if a thirty- or sixty-minute summary talk could be developed for use in such public venues as lectures, sermons and luncheons. Those several individual talks were jointly titled "How to Get the Family You've Always Wanted." This concept served as the abbreviated, popularized version of graduate school lectures, extended seminars and eventually the defining concept of this book.

Why This Book Is Needed

Families everywhere dream of having a good—even great—family. Yet, despite this incredible hope, the dream too often remains an unfulfilled fantasy because parents as leaders of the family do not know the steps, stages or tools to fulfill the dream. This book can give tools to your family to make the dream reality.

The second reason this book is needed is the uniqueness of its five-model approach. Most books attempt to sell you on just one model—the author's proven approach. *How to Get the Family You've Always Wanted* takes into account that families are uniquely different from one another and that different stages in a family's development may require inclusion of principles from different models.

The third reason is that this book can assist families in the balancing act of living life. Sustaining faith and hope, implementing discipline and boundaries, and developing a structure of some sort are all difficult. Sometimes it's hard to remember to have fun and enjoy one another in the process.

Finally, the approaches put forth in this book are realistic and workable; common-sense and experiential; and proven by clear and achievable outcomes. This book will help you dream a dream, create the plan to achieve that dream and work successfully toward the outcomes.

The Biblical Basis of the Family

I'm fascinated by people who espouse the "biblical family." There actually is very little in Scripture about how to create one. I'm also discovering that much of what is taught is either common sense or a baptized, cultural version that we call "Christian." But is it specifically, uniquely Christian? If what is being regarded as "biblical family" actually is true to biblical principles, then it seems there would be more congruence in form and model among cultures, regions and theological understandings.

The Bible does give us some tools for discipling, empowering and blessing families, whether within our own families or in our communities of faith. So what is the big picture?

Throughout this book I will give you very few "shoulds" for your family. Rather, I'll help you discover what you want your family to look like. What are your options from Scripture so that you can create a congruent plan for your family?

Foundations of Family

Deuteronomy 6 is one of the classic passages regarding families in Scripture. In the midst of God giving the Law to Israel, He states,

"Pass this on to your families." God makes this really significant declaration, in essence: "Impress these things I have given you upon your children. Talk about them when you're at home, when you walk down the road, when you lie down, when you rise up—in all facets of life. Tie some symbols upon your hands, bind them upon your foreheads, write them on the doorframes of the house, and on the gates" (6:7-9).

God is not referring to a variety of Christian plaques with Scripture verses posted strategically in family bathrooms. God is saying to Israel that truth has to come to life somehow within the family. Don't just teach the truth in your family; make it live! Show them the truth—when you're hanging around your house, walking down the road, getting up in the morning, going to bed at night. In the Christian Church across North America, we've made the assumption that if we give people truth, then transformation just happens. Truth is not necessarily transformational for many families. Most of us know much better than we live.

So what does a family of faith look like for you? How do you energize a lifestyle of faith in which each person is motivated to say, "We want to be a family of faith?" Children have very different approaches to life and faith, so their questions are very different. How do you make faith live for each of them? This is so important, because if you can't make it live within the family, you can't make it live in a sanctuary.

One thing we decided to do a long time ago was to figure out how to make faith work when we were riding in a vehicle, seemingly forever. How would we do it when we were traveling down the road, when we were stuck in traffic? While living in Saskatchewan, we drove 18,000 kilometers together in a van one summer, and for the most part we liked one another at the end. We had to figure out how to make it work, especially because we had nine- and-a-half years' difference between the ages of the oldest and youngest child. So how do you make faith live when you've spent fourteen hours or more a day in a vehicle together and you have at least one child with Attention Deficit Disorder (or maybe two)?

How do you live through life's various stages? Whether the stage is toddler, elementary age or teens, what happens to your family at each stage? The variables are different all the time. Just when you think you have the pattern set, the variables change. That's a challenge. So let's discuss how you make personal and spiritual family development happen, not just in the fun times of life, but in all of the times of life.

In Joshua 24:15, Joshua makes his great declaration to all of Israel, saying, in essence, "It's time to decide what kind of families you will have. But as for me and my household, we really are going to serve the Lord."

I always find it interesting when a family member, particularly a patriarch, and more particularly a preacher dad, speaks for an entire family. Then during the week the kids say, "Dad, we don't think we're doing as a family what you said on Sunday." This always is humbling to the preacher dad.

I often hear kids say, "My parents are so angry."

And I say, "Wait a minute, I know your parents. They are the nicest people I know."

"Yeah, when you're around. You should see them when you're not around."

So I ask the kids, "Can I talk to your parents?"

"Yeah, but will I get in trouble?"

"Well, probably, but we also can get to the bottom of it or at least figure out part of it."

So I talk to the parents: "What's going on? You're the nicest people I know."

The story from the dad is almost always the same: "You know, we have this dream of what we want our family to be like, but it's hardly ever that way. I think what happens is that I get so intense, just because it's just so frustrating that it's not going the way I want it to. I express this feeling that looks like anger to the kids."

Then there are usually tears from the mom, who says, "I had a dream of a great family, and we are not accomplishing it."

Look at Ephesians 6. In our studies of Scripture, we typically segment and compartmentalize Scripture very well, often pulling out a verse or sometimes even a paragraph. So to understand chapter 6, begin at Ephesians 4:1, and remember, this is a letter. In Ephesians 4:1, Paul sets the pattern for the entire second half of the letter when he says, "I urge you to live a life worthy of the calling you have received."

One of the primary teachings of Scripture, both Old and New Testaments, is that we live a life worthy of our calling. In doing so, we try to reflect the very nature of God, the character of Christ, and represent that to each other. This concept is so crucial when we talk about how we represent God to each other in our families. It's the essence of a covenant understanding.

The whole last half of the book of Ephesians clarifies this. In chapters 4 and 5, Paul outlines four different movements:

- In chapter 5, he starts off by saying, "Be imitators of God" (5:1).
- In chapter 5, verse 2, he says "Live a life of love."
- He goes on in verse 8 to talk about how to live as children of light.
- In verse 15, he says to be careful of how we live—not as unwise but as wise.

And then in verse 21, he makes his summary statement for the whole chapter and a half: "Submit to one another out of reverence for Christ."

We often pick up on verse 22 and make it the primary teaching for families: "Wives, submit to your husbands as to the Lord." But this is just one of the applications. Paul talks to wives; he talks to husbands; he talks to slaves; and he talks to children. He gives the applications of verse 21—how we submit to one another out of reverence for Christ.

The concept that the biblical view of family is about authority is only one way to look at Scripture. As we look at the totality of the Old and New Testaments, we find a second model for family, a covenant approach in which families make agreements to live together in harmony and seek to represent God to one another.

"Covenant" means an agreement between at least two parties. It is more than a commitment, but not a contract. "Contract" implies a lack of trust. So always built into a covenant are a stronger party and a weaker party. In a covenant, both parties give their best—strength, commitment and faithfulness.

When you enter into a covenant with God, it's important to clarify that you are always the weaker party. We have to clarify that because there are people who say to God, "I don't want to do that; don't ask me to do this; no, I won't." The servant never says no to the master! If we have a tendency to do that with God, we should not wonder why our families sometimes do that with us.

So in 5:22 Paul makes an application to wives and what it means to submit to one another out of reverence to Christ. Then in verse 25, the application is to husbands about how they are to live this out. And then in chapter 6 the application to children is, "Honor your parents," which is going to look different in different cultures.

In 6:4, a key phrase appears about raising families: "Bring them up in the training and instruction of the Lord." I have been in churches where they've posted this verse in the educational wing as a philosophy. I think to myself, *You left out the first part of verse 4: "Fathers, do not exasperate [i.e., annoy] your children."*

Remember, the job of family is to represent God to one another, not simply to create structures and put demands on children so they end up saying, "Look, I don't really like you or your God." It's not about how hard you discipline or how well they obey. It is about how you live in reverence of Christ; how you walk worthy of your calling in Christ; how you model that for your families. So this whole second half of Ephesians says to fathers, "Look, you are representing God."

So don't just be strong in the discipline and instructions of the Lord; don't annoy or exasperate your children. If your children clench their fists out of exasperation and let out a big sigh and roll their eyes, something is wrong at home. It may have nothing to do with your child's being strong-willed. It may be that you need to learn how to represent Christ better to your family.

As I listen to people in the community of faith talk about family structures, the focus often is on responsibility and authority. Much of the teachings in the Church have focused just on those aspects rather than on relationships. Why have we done that when there is so much more in Scripture about relationships? Both the Old and New Testaments were written in the context of relationally based cultures.

Why did we, primarily in North America, begin to teach about structures?

Historic Foundations

Let's discover some key historic foundations of family. The first term to notice is *clan*. It's what Joshua refers to when he says, "As for me and my household [my clan], we will serve the LORD" (24:15). The clan represents a particular family unit, a dramatically extended family. A clan often extends beyond blood relatives. The concept of a clan has varied somewhat in different cultures and different eras. Extended families take in aunts, uncles, grandparents, cousins—several generations. Throughout history they have been cornerstones of families and family spiritual formation. Simply observe how the hand of God's blessing rests upon families and extended families for generations.

The second concept to address is generational blessing. What can this generational blessing look like, and how far does it go? A few years ago, my youngest son, Eric, who was about twenty at the time, said, "Dad, I want to talk to you about God's hand of blessing on our family. I know you and Mom talk about how you are first-generation people of faith. But I've been thinking about it; there has to have been lots of faith in our background. It's almost as if God's hand of blessing is too strong on our family for it to have started with you and Mom."

I replied that there might have been people we don't know of. But clearly, in Dianna's family and probably on my side as well, as far as we know, we were first-generation Christians.

My son just shook his head and said, "I gotta do some work on this, because it just seems too strong to have started a few years ago. Dad, did you ever think that maybe your job was to get it started in our family?"

There was this long pause. I asked, "What do you mean?"

He said, "Come on, look at Bo and me. I mean, we really have it. We can take this thing someplace. Dad, you're pretty good, but come on, maybe your job from God's perspective was just to kind of get it rolling in our family, because we really have it." He could see the power of blessing for our extended family for generations to come.

Here it also might be helpful to mention the numerous examples of the apprentice model in the Old Testament—a young person learned a trade, faith or family life from an intentional relationship within the extended family structure. The child typically was apprenticed not to a parent but to one of the parents' siblings (an uncle, for example). Depending on the time in history and the culture, the relative was sometimes the mother's brother or an uncle in a different way. He would then mentor the child.

One of the challenges of the apprentice model (as noted with Abraham and Lot) was that mentors never knew at what point to bless the apprentices to go off on their own. The apprentice often had to wait until the sponsor or master grew very old, became ill or even died. And sometimes that was much longer than individuals wanted to wait. But in the historic foundations of family, the individual's desires were secondary to the family.

NT Families Followed OT Traditions

Very little actually is recorded for us in the New Testament regarding families. But well-intentioned Christians will insist, "We are going to have a biblical family." I inquire about the type. "The kind where you stone your children when they're disobedient? The kind where you add multiple spouses? Which kind of biblical family are you hoping for?" There is very little said in the Bible about what God expects families to look like in today's culture with the exception of the covenant. But let's look at what we do have.

New Testament terminology is almost identical to Old Testament terminology: *house, family, clan*. But in the New Testament, as we saw particularly in Ephesians 4–6 (picking up especially on Ephesians 5:21), family is really a pattern of God's love, forgiveness and long-suffering. Family is a continuation of a covenant understanding (see Balswick and Balswick, *The Family*, in the bibliography).

Please capture this concept: Family is a place of mutuality. Fathers, do not exasperate your children; husbands, love your wives the way

Christ loved and gave Himself for the Church. Family is a place of mutual respect, mutual submission and mutual blessing!

There are some unique Old Testament cultural twists on family. Polygamy, for example, is introduced in Genesis 4. I am fascinated by time frames in Scripture. In Genesis 2 we have creation accounts. Creation was a significant event in human history. By God's design, family is to be one man, one woman forever. Two chapters later, in Genesis 4, a man asked, "May I have two women?" Please notice a few things: It's only two chapters after creation, and it's not a woman saying, "Can I have two of those guys?" It is a man saying, "May I have two women, please?"

God answers, "If you are going to have multiple spouses, multiple wives, will you take good care of them and the children? Because I hate it when anyone is oppressed." You see, what matters in the heart of God is not always proper behavior, because His grace extends to the end of people's lives; He wants to redeem all of them. So God says, "If you're going to do this, will you at least take good care of them?"

Notice that polygamy and bigamy were rare, limited to the wealthy and the rulers. They had to have money to support their wives, and they had to have large houses so there could be peace. Commoners were always monogamous for financial and other reasons. Monogamy was praised. And note that Solomon and his harems mark a decline in the nation of Israel.

Extended families were the norm in the Old Testament. What's more, they were not defined by blood only. Extended families included aunts, uncles, servants and concubines. How did they get in there? Because God's blessing rests upon them as well. Often they were not willing participants. They were forced in, bought in, sold in. Even travelers and prisoners came under the Abrahamic covenant.

The great power of families is to bless other families in the community. The goal of family is keep all your members tight and together and to be agents of God's grace. Therefore, single people can use their homes as agents of God's grace. Childless couples whose hearts ache have a chance to be blessings to other families. Grandparents who were less than wonderful parents have a chance to be a blessing.

How many people, when you listen to their life stories, talk about the influence of a caring or a praying grandparent?

Traditional, Biblical, Modern and Postmodern Families

Traditional, biblical, modern and postmodern perspectives on family approach key concepts from incredibly different points. This is particularly true concerning commitment. In traditional marriages you have commitment to the institution. In the biblical model the covenant commitment between partners is most important. In modern families commitment takes the form of a contract; thus we have prenuptial contracts. If one does not fulfill his or her end, the agreement is broken.

The other divergent point to address is authority. In a traditional family model you can have male, even authoritarian, headship. The men typically are not abusive but can become quite dominant, depending on the culture and era. In the biblical concept of covenant, you have mutual submission and interdependence. In modern family structures, in contrast to both, you can have an absence of authority and no limited submissiveness. Some traditional models create a male-centered model of authority. The biblical covenant is relationship-centered. The modern model tends toward a self-centered perspective.

The research on postmodern families is in the early stages of development. Current anecdotes will soon lead to trends and patterns. In postmodern families marriage is not the initial commitment, as has been the pattern in traditional family worldviews. Now marriage is the icing on the cake. After a couple has been together for several years and even has had children together, they work toward solidifying a relationship so that a marriage can last for life.

Because marriage is something the couple is building toward when they are sure they can accomplish it, the official ceremony cements the family's relationship. This differs from setting the marriage up in the beginning and then trying to live it out. Postmodern families represent a significant cultural shift. Churches and communities of faith will need to coach couples and families toward their dream of a lifelong commitment.

Conclusion

In the quest for a truly biblical family, realize how different healthy families can look from each other and from culture to culture. I once taught a family life conference to a Chinese audience in Vancouver, British Columbia. All week they kept raising the question: In a Chinese family how long do you have to obey your parents? (see Ephesians 6:1). After repeated questioning, someone finally said, "You obey your parents the entirety of your life until they die." Someone else responded, "No, you obey your parents until you die." Apparently this is because the words of your Asian parents never leave you, and you don't want to disappoint them.

Families who embrace a developmental model would take the word *obey* and see it more in the context of "honoring" parents and parental wishes as the child enters young adulthood. The honoring would be understood by both parents and children so that parents would not want to impose their will, but offer perspective. Young adult children would respect their parents' wisdom, often asking for parental perspective or feedback. When a family has spent years in a developmental model, an empowerment model or a covenant model, these are normative conversations because you have represented God to one another in so many ways that mutual respect is a natural outcome.

Develop a biblical family, but realize that the more subtle presuppositions of region, culture and personal preference probably can and will influence your understanding of family and the corresponding outcome of your family.

CHAPTER 1

Developing the Family You've Always Wanted

When I became a professor in Canada, I was only thirty-two, but I had a thirteen-year-old son and a twelve-year-old daughter. My wife Dianna and I were looking at the parenting transitions between childhood and the teen years. I decided to survey a few hundred college students between the ages of eighteen and twenty-three to ask them general and a few developmental questions about their families. I was looking forward to insights we could use in our family to help our kids make the transition into their teen years and then, in just a few more years, into young adulthood.

The general responses were fascinating, especially the ones about spiritual development. Approximately twenty percent of the students had positive memories and feelings about spiritual development and family devotional times. Eighty percent of the students felt that either something was significantly lacking in that area, or they gave negative responses.

One twenty-year-old, a son of missionary parents, said the phrase he remembered most from family devotional times was, "John, would you please just shut up so we can get through this!" As you can guess, he did not have positive feelings about family devotions. But what intrigued me most was that his family kept having them. They didn't quit. On the one hand, I commend them for not giving up. On the other hand, I wondered why they didn't change the form or the structure of the devotions. Why not try something different? Why keep doing the same thing and expecting a different result?

Developing the Family You've Always Wanted

In order to have the sharpest, most well-defined target to aim at, begin with a clear focus. Start with a series of questions:

1. *What kind of family do we want?* Start with the goal in mind. Many of us haven't done that. Often we start with a series of "shoulds." Families often say, "We should really pray more as a family." Possibly, but isn't that obvious? I seldom hear anyone say, "I think the problem with our family is that we pray too much."

People, especially church people, have all sorts of unfulfilled shoulds. Much of the literature on Christian counseling will report that guilt resolution is one of the biggest issues Christian counselors face. They also report that one of the biggest issues of guilt motivation is living with unfulfilled shoulds. So seek to limit the shoulds in your life, and begin to discover what you want family to look like for you personally. If you are single, if you're just starting a family, if you're hoping your family will be different, what are you aiming for?

We discovered a long time ago that we were not a traditional family. We discovered very quickly that we were quite different from many families—and wanted to be. So we gave ourselves permission to be different and to enjoy the uniqueness. Although we fit many of the demographics of a classic family, we didn't fit the psychographics. Demographics give you objective criteria—number of people in the family, education, income, etc. Psychographics are the factors of psychological motivation—the things that inspire you to buy certain things, have certain values, decide what you do with those items and so on.

Imagine if your family had permission to be different instead of trying to fulfill "shoulds" that someone else puts on you. Take some time to dream your dream. Ask God, "What kind of people could we be; what kind of family could we become?"

2. What kinds of families have we seen? Most of the time we replicate what we've seen. Sometimes we say to ourselves, *I definitely do not want to be the kind of parent I've seen!*

Recently, I interviewed two pastors, one who ministers near a university, the other near a large Christian college. I asked them to describe the kinds of people that come in to them to be married and what kinds of premarital issues they address. After listening to them and studying the literature on this topic, I learned that of the couples united in marriage in the last five years in North America, less than twenty percent—some will say less than fifteen percent—say they've never seen a model of marriage they want to own themselves. Now that tells you a lot!

> Imagine if your family had permission to be different instead of trying to fulfill "shoulds" that someone else puts on you. Take some time to dream your dream. Ask God, "What kind of people could we be; what kind of family could we become?"

I was recently in a church of 400 people where the pastor was sharing about great difficulties in the marriages of that congregation. I suggested he create some marriage mentors. I requested the names of three to five couples who have a good family life. After a long pause, he said, "I can't come up with one, not one couple." That's not just bad news; that is something we have to address in this culture. It is imperative to ask, Why is this the case, and what do we do about it?

You have to start with the question, What kind of people are we? For some of you, it will require a clinician and some assessments to figure out what kind of people you really are. Don't try to be something you're not. You can only choose the kind of discipleship model that is going to work best for you if you know who you are.

3. *What kind of model best suits us?* Once you have a good idea of the kind of person you are and the kind of family you want to develop, then consider the kind of structure that will work best. Models can be as varied as people. Some are brief but meaningful. Some are large and elaborate. Some are smooth and take little to implement, while others are so detailed it takes a corporation to run the family. These five models of coaching your family have arisen from my experience observing, mentoring, counseling and coaching thousands of leaders and their families. The five models include:

- The **high-structure model**, for those who function best with form and detail.
- The **relational model**, which is a uniquely love-based, limited structure but high on caring and being together.
- The Christian **lifestyle model**, in which a family chooses a particular approach, set of values or outward image of the kind of family they want to be. Often attention is focused far more on outward forms and appearances than on internal values and nurturing relationships.
- **Covenant model**. Regardless of the type of faith in the covenant model—whether Protestant, Catholic or Jewish—the family members simply represent God to one another. The family determines the images and values of God they most value and then reflects those values within the family.
- **Integrative structures approach**. In this model families emphasize how to live out and experience their dreams as they move along throughout life. The integrative model is very experiential. All of life is an arena for teaching, modeling and being family together.

4. *What do we do with all the leftover stuff?* It's great to have a dream and necessary to make it as clear as possible. Families develop well when they can celebrate their successes and move to the next level of effectiveness. However, it's also necessary to deal honestly and directly with anything that keeps the dream out of reach or that will sabotage the desired outcome. Day-to-day human stuff will be addressed in chapter 6. It's time to honestly address certain issues, because any single one of these can derail the dream you have for your family:

- Fantasy without corresponding discipline and follow-through.
- Too much idealism, rigidity, pressure.
- Irresponsible reactions of anger, blaming, resentment, bitterness, unforgiveness.
- Unacceptable practices of violence, cheating, lying, stealing, unfaithfulness.
- The hopelessness issues of panic, anxiety, depression, emotional deprivations.
- The darkest stuff like family myths, family lies, family secrets and abuse that too often are not mentioned in the light of day.

5. *Where do we start?* The key to coaching your family toward a desired outcome is first to make a commitment to begin and stick to it. Next, create a working plan, have a clear focus and keep the end in mind. Finally, create clear steps and stages to reach the dream, celebrating successes along the way and refocusing the plan as you move toward the goal.

Desired Outcomes

To effectively coach your family's development, a key consideration is simply to ask:

- What do we want the outcomes to be?
- What kind of family life do we want?
- What kind of focus do we want our family to live out?
- When we have done this for five or ten or twenty years, what do we want the outcomes to be?

Too often families do not consider specific outcomes but simply make general comments like, "We want to have a good family. We want to have a family of faith. We want to have a healthy family." So let's create a working definition of coaching your family and do an overview of coaching models.

Definition of "Coaching Your Family"

Coaching your family is a relational process whereby people (parents and extended family) seek to intentionally develop the members of the family through each stage of life from birth on, individually empowering them to put to use the best of each person's strengths and character. Together, they commit their lives as a collective unit that will pass on the best of who family is to the next generation.

In the coaching process, it is essential to understand how people move through developmental processes, from their current point to the point where they want to be. The coaching process will include spiritual development but also the issues of trust, love and affirmation that are built into a person's life.

In this approach to the coaching process, people often move naturally from one stage to the next. But also be aware that sometimes people get stuck at a particular point and need specific encouragement, nurturing or even a specific experience in order to move to the next stage. It seems to work best if family members can help one another keep perspective and anticipate what the next stage of development might be. As much as possible they should seek to feed one another's dreams rather than react to current behaviors that seem to be difficult to tolerate. Ultimately, the developmental process of coaching is to focus on long-term outcomes rather than short-term behaviors.

Models of Coaching Your Family

High-Structure Model. The high-structure model is content-oriented. Ephesians 6:4 often is used as guidance: Raise your children in the discipline and the instruction of the Lord. Emphasis is on regularity and consistency. Devotional times are most often regular and consistent with significant input of biblical content. Spiritual development and serving in ministry all have structure to them. The high-structured discipleship model works well for high-structured people and families. It works well with families who have a particular lifestyle. High-structure family discipleship is a great model for those people who can make it work. But if you are not a person who can make high-structure work, then do not despair. There may be a more effective model for you.

Relational Model. Love is the primary focus of the relational model. The family keeps returning to this base again and again. It's talked about, it's modeled, it's shown, it's felt and it's valued. In a relational model, not only do individuals interact well with each other, but they also interact well within larger family systems: extended family, aunts, uncles, grandparents, etc. At an early age children learn to interact verbally and relationally with people of various ages. The emphasis is on time spent together. Families do things and interact together—for example, going out with two or three people, fishing or cross-county skiing together or going to a favorite restaurant where special conversations will take place. In these relationships faith is built and depth is developed. Although the structures do not appear to be obvious, these are foundational structures that connect people to each member of the family and, ultimately, to God.

Christian Lifestyle Model. In this model the family displays the Christian lifestyle. Image is crucial, and conforming to that image is expected. That may sound negative, but it doesn't need to be. With this model certain things are expected. And although other families will do it differently and children may argue, "Other families don't have to do this," or "Why doesn't their family do this?" the simple response would be, "In this family, this is how it is. This is what is expected, and this is how we treat each other."

As part of this Christian lifestyle model, there is limited developmental focus on heart and soul issues and more focus on simply being Christians together. Discussions often don't go deeply into why things are done the way they are. Simply, within the individual family this is how things are done. From an outsider's perspective it is fascinating to watch these families operate. When it is done well, they make it look so easy. It can appear as though there are very few problems. The limitation to this model is twofold: (1) The lack of the intentional development of individuals within the family, and (2) evidence from individuals who state, "I came from a Christian family." There is usually a pause and then a "but," and then they continue to say, "There was not a lot of depth in teaching, but it was a really good family."

Covenant Model. The covenant model seems to be used widely in the Old Testament. In *The Family: A Christian Perspective on the Contemporary Home*, Jack and Judith Balswick document the use of the covenant model of family in the Old Testament. In this model the goal of the family is to represent God to one another. Pause for a moment and begin to make a list of the characteristics people appreciate most about God. The list might include:

- God is always there.
- God is committed to us.
- God offers grace, understanding and forgiveness.
- God is faithful.
- God is strong.
- God provides security.

That is also a picture of how humans can represent God to one another. In the covenant model, the role of the stronger party is to empower the weaker party so that each person can move to the next level in the development of their faith. There is encouragement to move on. There is structure when structure is needed. There is grace when grace is needed. There is a high level of intimacy. Within the covenant, there is a strong commitment to each member of the family. It's a great picture of how the family can be a unit, where all the best of God is represented by each family member.

Integrative Structures Model. In the family that demonstrates the integrated model, there is less focus on biblical content and Christian "stuff." The emphasis is on living out a practical understanding of faith. For example, rather than sitting down for family devotions and having a structured time, a family may pick a passage in Scripture and spend an extended time acting it out, creating costumes and making it a full-scale production. In this way the family members are learning more than content alone. They are having fun as a family, living out their faith, creating this demonstration of faith and bringing the Scriptures to life. Conversations and family structures revolve around day-to-day living. These families engage in real-life conversations. The key is asking reflective and developmental questions.

There is less focus on behavior and biblical content and more emphasis on how people actually live out their faith. Parents seek to identify areas of strength and passion in each family member and then help each other live those out. You feed the dreams of each person in your family. Within the family unit there is strength, encouragement and hope. The clear focus of the integrative framework is taking a few basics of the Christian life and really living them out well together.

All five of these models all have strengths, and all have a few inherent weaknesses. There are three questions to consider as a family looks at discipleship models:

1. What is the desired outcome for the family?

2. What style best fits the family?

3. What things can the family put to use that they already do well?

Integrate those with the existing structure rather than trying to create something new. Ask God for a sense of which model can work best for your family.

Developing an Approach to Coaching Your Family

After looking at various models of development, note that no one style of family development will work for all people. So where do you start? Begin with a commitment to both start and follow through. Start small rather than big. Start with the end in mind and think about outcomes. Use as little or as much structure as needed, but do not let the structure drive the process. Take time to talk with each member of your family, and take time to pray for each member of your family. Take time to listen well. Remember to speak words of empowerment, encouragement and affirmation. Remind family members of God's gifts to them; remind them of their natural strengths and the gifts that make them unique. Remind them of the things they do well. Coach and encourage them on how to be even more effective as they live their lives. Paint a verbal picture for them of ways God can use the family in the future. Take time to represent God to one another.

It is true that we can never take a snapshot of our families at any given time and declare, "This is our family." On any given day a picture simply reflects what our families are like today. There are too many variables in life that come our way to feel either too secure on one hand or too hopeless on the other hand.

Dianna and I decided many years ago that we wanted to experiment with family structures. My father was an inventor/designer who never did anything the way it had always been done. He was always looking for another way to accomplish almost everything. We decided to do that with our family when our children were very young, knowing that some things would work quite well and a few experiments might fail. We brought the children into the process so they were fully aware that they were guinea pigs.

Through the years a number of incidents indicated that this approach may not have been a good idea. As each of the children went away to college, he or she would return home and announce that although the process had worked well on him or her, it obviously was not working on the younger siblings. I would often remind them that taking a picture of the family at any given time only gives you the image and status of that day.

At the time of this writing, all four of our children are in their young adult years. One can always wish a few things were different, and the ideal is yet to be attained, but the big picture looks quite good from the lens and angle I'm using today. We've come close to the desired outcome we established more than twenty-five years ago. It has been an enjoyable journey, filled with unexpected setbacks and amazing experiences. But the final chapters of our family's story are yet to be written, and the next generation soon will begin their own stories. Dream a dream for your family. Generations to come will thank you—and tell stories of your life.

For Review, Reflection and Action

Key Thoughts of the Chapter

1. The five diagnostic questions of your family:
   a. What kind of family do we want?
   b. What kinds of families have we seen?
   c. What kind of model best suits us?
   d. What do we do with all the leftover stuff?
   e. Where do we start?
2. Introduction to the five models of coaching your family:
   a. High-structure model
   b. Relational model
   c. Christian lifestyle model
   d. Covenant model
   e. Integrative structures model
3. Create a model that is "you" and commit to getting started!

Questions for Further Discussion

1. As you start to think about the kind of family you want, what are the two key ingredients you would like to include at that start?
2. Think of your family of origin and identify two elements of that family you might like to include in your own family and one or two elements you would like to be sure not to include.
3. When you write the last chapter of your family's story, what would you like it to say?

Action Plan

1. Begin to identify any leftover stuff in your life and family that could sabotage this process.
2. Identify your two first steps to get a working plan of family started.

CHAPTER 2

Determining Your Desired Outcomes

One of my favorite special-event sermons uses the example of the beheading of John the Baptist. I usually deliver this sermon on Mother's Day. The connection between a beheading and Mother's Day may not strike you immediately, but there is a powerful message for every person: We all have the opportunity to pass on something special to those we love.

As the story unfolds (see Matthew 14:1-12; Mark 6:14-29), Salome, Herodias's daughter, dances for Herod the Tetrarch on his birthday. Suitably impressed, Herod impulsively offers his stepdaughter anything she wishes, up to half his kingdom. Surprised, the young dancer consults her mother for advice. At that moment Herodias has a choice. This is the opportunity of a lifetime for her daughter. She could influence her daughter in such a way that Salome could receive a blessing that would carry her for the rest of her life. Herodias's decision, however, did not pass on the blessing. Rather, she requested the head of John the Baptist on a platter, which passed on her own bitterness to the next generation.

Although our lives often are not nearly as dramatic as this, our stories play out much the same way: We all have the opportunity to pass on blessing or our own bitterness to the next generation. The key to coaching your family is to determine what outcomes you want.

When you start this process, be sure to include both objective and subjective criteria with measurable outcomes.

Objective criteria may revolve around
- Educational status.
- Income and desired standards of living.
- Hometown and even street address.
- Community, church, club involvement, etc.

Subjective criteria will include
- How you spend the available income.
- Ways you will enjoy your standard of living.
- How much of your personal wealth you keep for yourself and how much is shared with others.
- How much your family laughs together, plays together and prays together.
- Shared levels of affection, intimacy and communication.

Begin to determine the desired direction and outcome for your family. Then make day-to-day decisions that will move your family toward the outcomes your family has determined for itself.

In my international work with emerging young leaders, I spend significant time with each person, both in the group and individually, coaching him on effective ways to reach his goals and, in the process, a balanced life. Many leaders are striving in the early stages of their professional development at the same time that they are working on the early stages of marriage and family. So there often are key points of tension and confusion. To assist them in this process, I introduce them to a few key models and reflective questions.

In many ways, developing the family you desire has significant similarities to models used to reach other seemingly unrelated goals. One such approach is similar to that which the National Aeronautics and Space Administration took in the 1960s to place the first people on the moon, an amazing feat of human ingenuity. The techniques are amazingly simple:

1. Begin with the desired outcome.
2. Break the overall process into steps or stages.
3. Determine what steps you already know and can implement successfully.
4. Begin to research and discover ways to effectively develop the steps or stages that currently are not as clear.
5. Determine reasonable time frames both for stage development and for the overall process.
6. Always keep the outcome in mind.
7. Make routine decisions that will help you reach the outcome.
8. Celebrate successes along the way.
9. Reach your goal, your desired outcome.
10. Fully celebrate the outcome. Enjoy!

Some of you may be feeling like this is a lot of work and planning for family! After all, isn't family about relationships? Shouldn't it be easier than this? Do I have to be an aeronautical engineer to coach my family? Not at all. But two keys are important to remember: First, if you have not been able to develop the healthy family you had dreamed of to this point, it probably will not mysteriously happen when you wake up one day next week. It will take a plan and some developmental steps. Second, consider how few worthwhile ventures in life happen automatically because of simple hope or desire. Some things happen that way. But if not, then typically a plan and intentional development are needed to reach the desired outcome, whether the issue is a retirement plan, a weight loss plan, home remodeling, additional education or recovery from an accident. This may be true of your family life as well.

AN APOLLO APPROACH TO FAMILY DEVELOPMENT

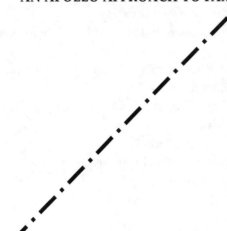

● **Stated Outcome/Goal**
- Healthy Relationships
- Identity: Personal and Sexual
- Confidence and Courage
- Affection and Intimacy
- Love and Security
- Connecting with God
- Disciplines: Personal and Spiritual
- Service and Outside Contributions
- Affirmation and Encouragement
- Communication and Hard Conversations

■ **Starting Point**

To assist in the process, ask some thoughtful, reflective questions. The Outcome Frame (see the work of Bandler, Gindler and Satir in *Changing with Families*) can help you clarify and discover implications for your family. Ask five Outcome Frame questions to assist you in continually clarifying where you are in the developmental process, what to adjust and what the next steps might be.

1. What is the goal or desired state? Describe what you want your life to be. Paint a picture with broad, sweeping strokes.

2. When, where and with whom do you want it?

3. How will you know when you get it?

4. How will your life be different?

5. What stops you from getting it? What do you need in order to get it?

These questions will assist your family in moving from a dream to reality by providing context, parameters, definitions of effectiveness and limitations.

Also consider:

1. Relationships you want to develop.

2. Experiences you want to have.

3. Situations you hope to influence.

4. Things you hope to be/do/have.

I can't emphasize it enough: Begin with the end in mind. Describe what the family you want will look like. Include a wide range of experiences, events, fun and feelings. Then plan ahead, because the experiences will change as people develop, mature and change. Be sure to consider the implications from items you include and from situations you may leave out. Create a desired outcome the whole family can embrace and enjoy.

Approaches to Family Coaching

There are several potential approaches to family development:

Disciplined and in control. Some parents and families, by their very natures, want (or even need) higher levels of control than others do for a number of reasons: It's what they are used to; it's what gives them a sense of security; it's a particular parenting philosophy; or they have a strong desire for their families to function in a particular kind of way. Strong parental controls and clear childlike obedience make this work.

Happy and empowered. A number of parents were children of the 1960s and found great comfort in the permissive society. They have articulated a parenting philosophy in which they don't say no to children any more often than necessary, if ever. They want to give family members a sense of freedom to explore and to be empowered. In small children this particular philosophy looks dangerous to some. But as children start school, they figure out that although their parents don't often say no to them, there are a number of other people in the world very willing to do so. Home then becomes a safe haven where dreams are nurtured and security abounds.

Limited embarrassment factor. Because I teach graduate family courses and work with leaders and their families, I try to keep up on literature about the family. I read through thirty to fifty new books every year on family-related topics. Last summer I read forty books on the family. I came to the conclusion that the summary statement of thirty-seven of the forty books could be, "If you follow these guidelines, you will not be embarrassed as the parent of your child."

I thought, *Isn't parenting, and discipleship in particular, more about the development of the children than the image of the parents?*

Dianna and I decided to take a very different approach. We made an assumption that our children would embarrass us, and that was OK. We had intentional conversations with our four children when each of them was sixteen and assured them that over the next few years they would make a number of mistakes. And we let them know that was OK. We gave them permission to fail, permission to try new things, permission even to embarrass us a bit. We talked about how to learn from mistakes. We assured them that we would rather be embarrassed by them and have them feel the freedom to work through things honestly than to put on an image that everything is OK. When considering outcomes, it's helpful to decide the importance of image versus honesty.

Life calling and lifestyle. There are actually two sides of this outcome. The first side has to do with the issue of success as defined by the family. All across North America, families work diligently to get their children into the right preschools so they can get them into the right kindergartens. They focus on good grades and performance so they can get them into the right prep schools, the right universities, the right professions. And some even make the assumption that if a child does not get into one of the top five or ten universities in the country and achieve an education that would gain entry into one of the top-salaried professions, then the family has not been successful in their quest. The goal is to have the lifestyle you desire.

> Herodias had a choice. She could influence her daughter in such a way that Salome could receive a blessing that would carry her for the rest of her life. Rather, she passed on her own bitterness to the next generation. We all have the opportunity to pass on blessing or our own bitterness to the next generation.

The other side of lifestyle and life calling has to do with being a model Christian. Here the family sees faith lived out in terms of individual gifts that are used: a lifestyle of evangelism; a lifestyle of caring, serving and giving. The children grow up in an environment where these values exist, then quite often value them in their future lives. On the one hand, life calling/lifestyle is about image and success. On the other, it's about character and value and how those values are modeled and lived out.

To have a family of faith. If faith has an outcome, the question has to be asked, "What kind of faith?" In some families of faith there is a lot of Bible knowledge. Children memorize Scripture passages early, then are involved in Bible quizzing. It is well known, however, that having Bible knowledge does not necessarily equate with effective family discipleship.

Other kinds of desired "faith" outcomes may be lifestyles of (1) prayer and (2) trusting in God alone. Another intentional "faith" outcome may be a family who sees its neighbors and friends being converted and coming to a personal faith in Christ. So rather than simply stating the desired outcome—having a family that loves God or a family of faith to pray, etc.—be more specific. What aspects of faith, what kinds of faith, are we looking at? How will faith be passed on?

Producing the next generation of adults. Children are viewed as children in this way of thinking. The emphasis is not on discipline, control or not being embarrassed by hair and clothing. The goal is to focus the family's discipleship efforts in such a way that the questions asked from very early ages are designed to help each member of the family move to the next developmental stage, knowing that outcomes will not be measured in the short term, but in the long term. With this perspective on outcomes, it becomes easier to look past annoying behavior at various stages and realize that each stage comes with its own challenge. However, each stage will change within a few months or years into yet another stage. Therefore, focus on the long run.

Some families do a very good job of coaching small children; others coach young teens well; some coach well during the high school years. The ultimate outcome, however, is that final stage of helping each member of the family move into a young adult faith and ultimately to an adult faith. Sometimes this does not happen well because the disciplining philosophy and practices are rooted in earlier stages or because of some image or lifestyle issue. The final outcome sees people of adult faith who reproduce that life of faith in another generation of believers.

It should be noted that none of these parenting approaches is necessarily more right or wrong or effective than the others. All have inherent strengths and weaknesses. The goal is to figure out what works for your family, what kind of people you are. Prayerfully consider what God would have you aim for in your family. Then systematically develop your strategy and implement it to achieve your desired outcomes.

For Review, Reflection and Action

Key Thoughts of the Chapter

1. In an Apollo approach to family development, you start with the end in mind, identify the steps or stages of development you know how to implement, and then work your way backward from the desired goal until you have created the necessary steps to reach that goal.

2. The Outcome Frame asks five reflective and diagnostic questions to assist you in developing a working plan of action for your family's development.
   a. What is the goal or desired state? Describe what you want your life to be. Paint a picture with broad, sweeping strokes.
   b. When, where and with whom do you want it?
   c. How will you know when you get it?
   d. How will your life be different?
   e. What stops you from getting it? What do you need in order to get it?

3. Six approaches are offered to assist you in the initial steps of framing your desired outcome of family:
   a. Disciplined and in control.
   b. Happy and empowered.
   c. Limited embarrassment factor.

    d. Life calling and lifestyle.

    e. To have a family of faith.

    f. Producing the next generation of adults.

Questions for Further Discussion

1. As you begin to create your dream or desired outcome, is it better for you to list objective descriptors of family, to think of specific relationships to be developed or to create a subjective picture of what you hope to see in your family?

2. Which of the six approaches to family do you feel most drawn to? Explain why.

3. If you were to pick one of the questions of the Outcome Frame that would be the most challenging for you to grasp or answer, which would it be? Explain why.

Action Plan

1. Begin to list items of your dream for your family in the Apollo Approach. What would be your top five words or phrases to incorporate?

2. In utilizing the Outcome Frame and the Apollo Approach, how is it best for you to dream your family dream? Use lists of words or phrases, relationship stories, specific experiences, word pictures or even a drawing or painting. Begin to clarify.

CHAPTER 3

Developing a Family Covenant:
Representing God to One Another

When our children were four and two, I had been with our four-year-old son and had dealt with him on several tough issues. Once when we sat down for our evening meal together, he looked up at me with his big, brown eyes and asked, "When I get big, will I be like you?"

The question hit me hard. I was not quite sure how to respond. After a long pause I answered him, "I'm not sure. Why? Do you want to be?" With a grin on his face he said, "Yes, Dad, when I get big I want to be just like you."

I was not prepared for that response. I thought, *He will be a lot like me*. Since that was the case I had to ask myself, *How do I want to be a father to him? What kind of family do we want? What do we want the outcomes to be?* In the twenty-five years since that day, we have dreamed our dream, created plans on how to fulfill it and celebrated the outcomes again and again.

Let's review a moment. To get the family you've always wanted, go back and ask those key reflective questions. Start with the end in mind—a goal, the desired outcome—instead of determining what you do not want your family to be like. What would you like your family to be?

Let's make the concept of family fairly broad. Single people are part of a family; people without children are part of a family; people who once were married and are not now are still family. Let's also look at nuclear family, extended family and the Church as a family of faith. Determine how you fit into family overall. Spell it out. Begin to determine what your family is going to look like once you "get there." Be as realistic as possible.

The next question is, What kinds of families have you seen? Most of the time we replicate what we've seen. Then ask, What kind of person am I? What kind of people are we? Sometimes we have an ideal in our mind that we cannot reach. So what kind of model of family coaching best suits you? What do you do with all the leftover stuff?

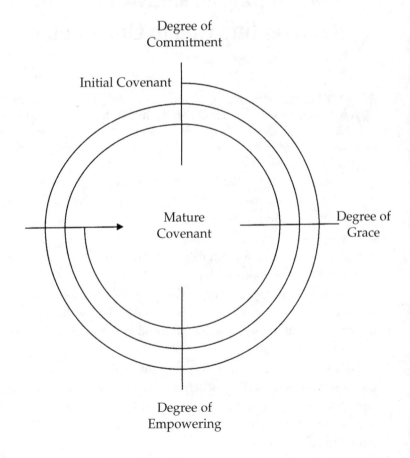

Allow me to explore the idea of the covenant model of family introduced earlier. In the covenant model, we start with a degree of commitment. An initial commitment, most often a marriage, is found in almost every cultural context. There is some sort of ceremony or something marking the beginning of two people coming together.

A review of the working definition of covenant is necessary as we delve deeper. The covenant model has an equally strong tradition in both the Old and New Testaments. A covenant is not a contract, because contracts relate to mistrust. A covenant is stronger than a commitment. It is really an agreement where two parties commit themselves to each other. There is always a stronger party and a weaker party in a covenant. So you have to remember that when you enter into a covenant with God, you are always the weaker party. In a covenant with God He gives you all of His strength and all of Himself. And in return God says, "I simply want you." That's it.

There is a degree of grace in a covenant understanding of family. In family situations somebody always has a need. If there are a number of children in the family, it's hard for everyone to be OK all at the same time. For that reason we can never take one snapshot of our families and say, "This is what our family is like." No, that's what our families are like *right now*. Things change. People make poor decisions. Outside influences come in and things you have no control over, like illness and disappointments, enter the picture. There will always be people in a family who need a little extra grace at a particular time.

Notice also the degree of empowerment in a covenant model. Families work so much better if we can understand how to give that power away rather than trying to control people. So many of the questions I receive at family seminars involve dealing with control. Most of the time I have to say, "You can't do anything about it." I have to say to parents, "Pray and trust God. Honestly, just keep silent." Families are to offer grace and empowerment to one another. Notice that saying what you want to say neither solves a situation nor improves it significantly. So it's probably not going to change much if you keep saying something to exercise power.

Also consider the degree of intimacy in a family, the sense of being understood, appreciated and valued simply for who you are. Intimacy empowers people in your family to move toward mature covenant. It gives people a sense that they belong.

What you're actually doing in a covenant-based family is representing God to one another. So let's look at how families in a covenant model do that. Peter gives us specific teaching on families. He tells us that in order to understand covenant in families, we have to understand the bigger picture about representing God to one another: "Just as he who called you is holy, so be holy in all you do; for it is written, 'Be holy, because I am holy'" (1 Peter 1:15–16). Let's back up to verses 13-14 where he talks about children in particular:

> Prepare your minds for action; be self-controlled; set your hope fully on the grace to be given you when Jesus Christ is revealed. As obedient children, do not conform to the evil desires you had when you lived in ignorance.

Families focus on the holiness aspect of God, primarily roles or authority or structures, as they live in harmony with one another in the covenant model. It logically follows then that family represents God. It is about how you set the tone, how you treat each other, ways you speak—literally, how you represent God to each other.

There are three key principles for us to see in Peter's writing: offer understanding, listen and bless.

Offer Understanding

Look at chapter 3, verse 6: "Sarah . . . obeyed Abraham and called him her master." Think about that; many men love that verse. From a male perspective it could be nice if all truth ended there. But it does not.

In verse 7, Peter begins, in essence, "Men, here is what I have to say to you"; then he gives three fairly brief but clear principles. The first one is: Offer understanding. Although he is speaking specifically here to men, these principles apply across the board to families. Verse 7 says, "Husbands, in the same way be considerate as you live with your wives, and treat them with respect." Pick up on the last phrase of this verse, "so that nothing will hinder your prayers." This could explain so much about church and faith, couldn't it? Men, live with your wives, with your families, in an understanding way so that your prayers will not be hindered. When I observe families interacting negatively, I wonder, *How can God's blessing rest upon this family in this place?*

I've learned so much over the years about offering understanding. It never came easily for me, nor does it for many of us. When our family was young, we developed what we called "family councils." We started them when the children were young and typically conducted them monthly or whenever the need arose. In family council anyone could bring any complaint he wanted to. So if there was a conflict during the week, we would bring it up at family council. That way we didn't have to get into arguments throughout the week. Any time something came up, we could simply remind the other person to hold off and bring it up at family council on Sunday night.

The patterns typically were the same. We would have a meal together and then start off with some words of affirmation for each other. Our youngest daughter enjoyed this most. She would repeatedly say, "I love everything about everybody." Once in particular, while we were living in Canada, our dream for our family was not materializing. So we declared a family council, a serious family council. We planned this one as a bigger event than usual. I thought, *Since I am the father of the family, I clearly understand what the problems are. It's just a matter of time before I get to clarify everyone's issues.*

So we sat down, did our obligatory affirmations and got started. The first child spoke, "Dad, you're always so intense and angry."

I'm thinking, *Yeah, yeah, yeah, whatever, that is not the issue here.*

And the second one spoke and said, "Yeah, Dad, I agree. You're the problem here."

I responded, "What, you didn't have a criticism of your own? So by the power of suggestion, you just picked up this one?"

She responded, "No, really, Dad. I've thought about it a lot. I think that is the issue of our family."

In silence I thought, *Whatever!*

The next one spoke, "Me too. I think that's the issue. Dad, it's you. It is you."

I simply responded, "OK, then you all have to work with me here, because I don't get this. I'm the nicest guy I know! Look at me; I'm a teddy bear. I'm nice; I don't yell; I certainly don't hit."

They responded, "True, but it's not yelling or hitting. You are tense, and it's that look."

And I said, "What look?"

They said, "That look!" and pointed at my expression.

In my defense I responded, "I've perfected the look so I don't have to yell and hit, so I get what I want."

Our oldest daughter said, "Dad, sometimes I've thought, when I've gone to my room, that it might almost be easier if you yelled or hit. That look is painful."

Again I said, "Then you guys have to help me. I've obviously really missed it." Then I remembered the First Peter passage and went and read it. The meaning sank in for me: "Men, live with your wives, with your families, in an understanding way so that your prayers will not be hindered." Whoa, I had missed it!

St. Francis said, "Seek not to be understood but to understand." What is one of the great things you love about God? He understands you, your uniquenesses, what you're like, your jerky side, your soft side. He understands you. In families, God's dream for us is that we understand each other.

I was the interim speaker for a few months at a church with a thousand people. It was a classic New England church—big windows floor to ceiling, white painted pews, big organ, huge pulpit. People considered themselves upper-middle-class, a little uppity. Yet I loved preaching there. My style annoyed them a bit. It was a fun challenge for all of us.

One Sunday after speaking, I was stopped by one of the men on the way out. He said, "Martin, I just want to challenge you. You are really good on the soft side of God, but you're not very good on judgment."

I inquired, "Was there any judgment in the passage I preached this morning?"

"Well, no."

I said, "OK, why would I preach judgment when it's not in the text? When I get to a text that has judgment, I will preach judgment. I'll preach it right at you if you would prefer. I will call you by name."

He responded, "I just wanted to mention this because it would appear that you are much better on the soft side of faith."

"May I ask you a few questions?" I said. "You like judgment, don't you?"

He said, "Yeah, I think it's very important."

"Do you have children?"

"Yes."

"They are probably grown, out of the home, aren't they? Do your children love God?"

He said, "They are having a hard time with God right now."

I paused and asked, "Do your children love you?"

With his head down he responded, "It's been tough lately."

> In a family we represent God to each other. Let's review the list: God cares, listens, loves, understands, forgives, empowers and is always there. That's what the people closest to you would love from you.

Then I kindly but firmly said to him, "Do not ever challenge me or anybody else again until you learn to live with your family in an understanding way and represent God to them. You may like judgment, but your family's eternity is hanging in the balance, and right now you are not representing God very well."

He left abrubtly. He did not thank me! I noticed over the next several weeks that he was not present in church. About three weeks later I stopped his wife and asked where he was. She said, "He's not been here. You are not his favorite person right now."

"I'm sure that's true. Send my greetings and hug him for me."

Two weeks later she stopped by and said, "I need to tell you something. In the last month I've seen my husband cry more than I have in thirty-five years of marriage. Something is happening to him. In the last few weeks he has written letters to all four of our children. Pray for us because today at 5 o'clock we're gathering as a family. It will be our first time together in seven years, and the kids are scared to death."

Live with your families in an understanding way so that your prayers will not be hindered because, like it or not, you represent God to the people closest to you. Represent God well!

Listen

A second principle in understanding family is the concept of listening. The principal is not as clearly stated in First Peter, but it is a natural application of living with families in an understanding way and representing God. In family literature about teenagers and their parents, the primary complaint of teenagers is, "My parents don't listen to me!"

Have you noticed that telling everyone what you think is not in high demand in most families? Not many people close to you sit around and request, "I would love to hear everything you think about my life." If they want coaching tips, they'll ask. Otherwise they aren't that interested in hearing all of your opinions.

A number of years ago I decided to do a survey. I was going to be speaking on how to show honor and respect in families. That's a natural process, or so I thought, although it is usually performance-based. Parents do it for children when children do well. People tend to do it for women, mothers mostly. But it was hard to figure out how families show honor or respect to men.

So I planned to interview fifty men. I strategically picked different kinds of men with different kinds of positions, from working men who had a variety of jobs to a number of executives. I even went into a prison and interviewed five prisoners. What I found was fascinating. I asked, "How does someone show honor or respect to you?" Forty-three of the fifty men said as their first or second response, "When someone listens to me."

I wasn't prepared for this. I got impassioned responses from men who said, "Do you have any idea how hard it is to get someone to listen to you?" Many answered, "Look, I'm the boss at work. Everybody wants something from me. Nobody ever asks about me. I go home and nobody ever asks about me. They want this or they need that from me. I'm always the giver! And no one listens to me."

I thought these were going to be very brief interviews. But some took two hours to listen to these men because no one else listened to them. Listening is a significant empowering principle in family.

Bless

The last principle about representing God to one another comes from First Peter 3:8–9:

> Finally, all of you [not just slaves, not just wives, not just husbands, all of you], live in harmony with one another; be sympathetic, love as brothers, be compassionate and humble. Do not repay evil with evil or insult with insult, but with blessing, because to this you were called so that you may inherit a blessing.

You have received the best of what the Father has to give to you. And in turn God wants you to pass that on to the people closest to you in the form of a blessing.

In conversations with hundreds and hundreds of parents who travel for a living, we have done a great deal of coaching as to how to parent when you are absent. Let me pass on a few recommendations on how to bless your family when you're away.

Before the age of instant technology was upon us, the first thing I did when I got to an airport or got on a plane was to write a short note, card or letter to my wife and each of our four kids. I carried supplies with me, including stamps, and often would write just a few lines and mail them either before I got on the plane or first thing when I landed. On a short trip I would get home before the letters did, but that did not reduce their impact. The last time we moved, the kids were all college-age or older. When they came back to clean out their rooms and their stuff, two of the kids showed me large shoeboxes of all the notes I had sent them. They said they kept them and have reread them on numerous occasions.

Now it's simple to keep very current with e-mail. The key to staying in touch through e-mail is not just doing factual connections but also to reflect on matters of the heart and to try to listen for emotion, as well as content.

Third, cell phones are great for keeping very current, whether it's in an airport, from a car or walking to a meeting. Keeping track of where the people of your family are at any time of day lets them know that they are thought of, remembered and cared for. Either leave them a voice mail or just give them a one-minute call.

These are ways to remember to take care of the little things. It's the little things that make the most difference, and there's great power in them. Remember, in a family we represent God to each other. Let's review the list of what we so appreciate about God: God cares, listens, loves, understands, forgives, empowers and is always there. That's what the people closest to you would love from you as you represent God to each other.

In our first year of living on the Canadian prairies, I was driving the three-hour trip between Regina and Saskatoon, Saskatchewan, and saw a number of unusual small, domed buildings. I had never seen anything like them before. I was so curious that I pulled off the highway down into a valley, into a group of these small structures. It was March on the prairies and dreadfully cold—minus thirty degrees centigrade with a strong wind. As I got out of my car and walked toward one of the buildings, I saw that no one was there, and I let myself inside.

As soon as I stepped in I discovered what it was—a unique Canadian prairie greenhouse unlike any I had ever seen. I stood there for a few minutes, and the marked contrast between standing inside and being outside in the cold struck me. That kind of cold could cause death in a short period of time. But inside it was 15° Celsius (60° Fahrenheit) with lots of humidity. It was an atmosphere absolutely conducive to the growth and development of young plants. Because the winters are so long in that part of Canada and because the soil takes so long to thaw, it's hard to put seeds into the ground and get them to germinate quickly.

Inside that greenhouse an overwhelming thought hit me: This is the exact analogy of what God wants our homes to be like. It's tough outside! The environment is more than challenging; it's lethal. But inside that greenhouse there was an atmosphere absolutely conducive to the growth and development of young plants.

Can we make a commitment and a plan so that home and family are safe places for growth and development? Can we develop this safe harbor not only when the children are young, but as each one of us goes through life?

For Review, Reflection and Action

Key Thoughts of the Chapter

1. The covenant model of family begins with an initial covenant between two parties or people and contains four key elements in order to produce a mature covenant:
   a. A degree of commitment.
   b. A degree of grace.
   c. A degree of empowerment.
   d. A degree of intimacy.
2. The covenant model of family can be summarized best as "In families we represent God to each other."
3. Remember the power of listening to each other. It is extremely empowering.
4. Remember the power of blessing one another in families.

Questions for Further Discussion

1. Within your current family structure, which individual(s) need extra empowerment? Extra grace? Extra intimacy?
2. On a scale of one to ten, how would you evaluate your current pattern of listening well to each other in your family? Which individuals need to listen more? Which individuals need to be listened to more? Which individuals present the greatest challenge to fulfilling their listening needs?
3. As you begin to identify your patterns of speaking blessings to each other, list one or two ways you do this best in your family.

Action Plan

List ways you currently represent God well to each other. Begin to list a few ways you could improve within your family at representing God to each other.

CHAPTER 4

When You Know It's Time to Change

Whether your family clearly is in a crisis or is simply experiencing a growing awareness of its needs, you may realize that it's time for a change. But immediately the questions and doubts start to come: Where do we start? How do we do it? What if it doesn't work? What if we can't? What if we can't agree on what to do? What if? . . .

For many of us, there is something we really want in life. We know it's good for us. We know it would be healthy and better, and yet there is something deep inside our psyches—something involving personal motivation—that keeps us from realizing the dream. That something stubbornly resists making the necessary change and embracing the thing that would be so good for us. This tendency is fascinating to observe and normative in the human experience.

Individuals may know on multiple levels that it's time for change. We may feel it deeply. There may be trusted people close to us whose advice and encouragement reinforce this sense that change is essential. Even though all of this may be true, still there is something inside us that resists making that needed change.

The pattern is quite common. We hear something, see something and even feel something—and it stirs us. Sometimes it even stirs us deeply. "It's time," we say. "OK, I'm going to do it. I need a change." We even may begin to "do it" for a short amount of time, but the change is not permanent. Before long, the motivation wanes and the perspective is lost.

To attain the desired outcome in your family will take more than a hope, a dream or even a plan. It will require extensive follow-through for the long run that entails asking, Why do people change or not change? What does it take to change?

Life-change is a multibillion-dollar industry in the United States. Think about it for a few moments. Consider the whole fitness craze. The rough statistics are that eighty percent of all fitness equipment is sold the two weeks before Christmas and the week between Christmas and New Year's Day. By Easter, eighty-five percent of the equipment is not used again. But it's not sold at garage sales the first year; that wouldn't be good stewardship. It's sold in the second and third year after it has collected dust and gotten a little rusty.

Another life-change emphasis is weight loss. Every little strip mall across North America has some sort of weight-loss clinic. You go to the bookstore and there are whole sections on diet and health. There is also rehab. If you can't do life-change for yourself, there's always a place you can go and commit yourself for three or four weeks, and they make you change.

If that doesn't work for you, there's always plastic surgery. You know it's part of a multibillion-dollar industry. And there's always the lottery. The odds are better that you'll get hit by lightning playing golf than win the money, but it's a chance for life-change for some of you.

As you can see, real life-change is hard to come by. Yet, the quest continues endlessly.

So what do we do when we know it is time for a change? Let's use a case story to help us learn the answer. Matthew records an account of a young man who came to Jesus to ask about the big questions of life—real questions about life and meaning and, ultimately, his soul. It's a story about life-change.

People Come Seeking

Look at Matthew 19:16. A young man with significant resources came to Jesus, asking about eternal life. He addressed Jesus as "Teacher" and seemed to recognize that Jesus was someone with keen insight into the big issues of life and the soul. The man made an assumption that Jesus had some wisdom or would be able to give some advice that could help him on his quest.

All sorts of people came seeking Jesus—those who wanted hope and help, who needed healing or who needed nothing short of a miracle. All kinds of people came, from the poor beggar to the rich young ruler; from women of bad reputation to the woman who had endless physical problems that no doctor could cure; from the lepers to the rich who owned huge amounts of land. They all came seeking Jesus. So it really does beg the question, Why Jesus? Why were so many otherwise reasonable people drawn to Jesus? What was it about Him? Well, He had this amazing reputation.

The rich man in Matthew 19 came seeking Jesus because of that reputation. What was—and is—that reputation? Jesus knows and delivers. It doesn't matter who you are and what you've done, what life circumstances you've been in or what you need. Now that's an amazing reputation!

Jesus had amazing authority and power as well. If you came and needed healing, He seemed to know what to do. No matter who you were or what you needed, Jesus seemed to have authority to take care of it: a dreaded, unknown illness; voices that wouldn't go away; or the problem of living in caves and not being able to wear clothes. Jesus knew and delivered; Jesus had authority and power.

One of my favorite Jesus stories is about the fellow who brought his little boy to see Jesus. The boy had seizures, and the man didn't know if it was a psychiatric or physiological problem, like epilepsy, or maybe demonic. So he took the boy to Jesus. During the trip, the boy lapsed into a seizure and the demons threw him into the fire. And what did Jesus do? Put out the fire? No, Jesus spoke the word, and whatever it was that gripped the boy broke, just like that (see Mark 9:14-32).

Jesus knew and He delivered. Authority and power. He also had insight and wisdom. Jesus could and can look into your soul at the hidden things and know exactly what you need. He knows your story. And despite this insight and wisdom, there's no harsh judgment but rather incredible compassion.

Another of the great stories is recorded in Mark 1:40-45. A man with leprosy came to Jesus on his knees and begged for healing. The Scriptures say Jesus had compassion on him and reached out and touched and healed him, just like that.

Now that's a reputation! And because of it, the rich young man came seeking Jesus. So what did this man come seeking? He came about two things: What do I do about life? And how do I change?

I have been fascinated by the deep conversations I've had with people around the world in some of the most unlikely contexts. Most often the talks have been at their initiation about the big issues of faith and personal issues of the soul. I've spoken with people in prisons and detention centers, people who had a few too many drinks in a bar, people fighting at wedding receptions, people fighting at family gatherings—

All sorts of people came seeking Jesus—those who wanted hope, help, healing, a miracle—from the poor beggar to the rich young ruler. No matter who you are, what you've done, what you need, Jesus knows and He delivers.

wherever people talk about life. With all of the "advice" that is out there, there seems to be a significant amount of confusion as well.

Deep in the hearts of all women and men, girls and boys, is this quest for an understanding of something beyond themselves. The ancient writer Augustine said, "Our hearts will not rest until they rest in Thee, O God."

This wealthy young man who came seeking Jesus was looking not only for wisdom and insight, but he clearly specified that he was looking for eternal life. He asked, "What must I do to inherit eternal life?" (Matthew 19:16, author's paraphrase). This was not a theoretical question. It was something he was passionately seeking to pursue for himself. Perhaps his desire came from a sense of absence of meaning in life. Perhaps it grew out of a sense of emptiness.

He was longing for satisfaction beyond what his financial resources had secured for him. He wanted something more than he had, and money was not going to do it for him. He had some emptiness or at least an empty spot that kept gnawing at him. In his mind, this new life that Jesus was talking about may well have been the answer for him.

People Will Listen for Insight

When we search for wisdom and insight, for help and hope, whether for family issues or for our own souls, we very often are on a quest for something deep. We are reaching out for something to satisfy a longing being stirred up inside us. At times we're not even able to articulate what we're hoping for. This man who came to Jesus was longing to be satisfied, to be freed, to find ultimate rest, satisfaction and peace in his soul. And he understood that the answer to this desire was relational—not something he could buy with his wealth. Knowing this, he sought Jesus. But he wasn't just looking for spiritual insight; he was looking for specific answers to his inquiry of how to change his life.

Jesus said to him, "Obey the commandments" (19:17).

The young man asked, "Which ones?" (19:18). One almost gets the sense that he didn't want the standard religious answers. He had grown up with Jewish law. He knew what the rabbis, the teachers of Judaism, were saying. The established religion of the day would have provided similar insight, but he had not gone to other rabbis. He had come to Jesus. He knew he could find life-change there. He wanted something not in the realm of religion, but something of the spirit, something deep within him, something to change his life. Jesus' reply is very interesting: Simply keep the commandments (see 19:19).

Apparently, Jesus was entirely aware of the young man's dilemma. Jesus' response was intended to bring the truth to this man. Jesus was alerting him that it wasn't about what he did, but who he was. Life-change is often less about what we do and more about changing who we are! Jesus knew what the man owned and what his life was like. But the man's response was, "I've done this. I've kept the commandments" (see 19:20).

What Happens When Change Seems Too Hard?

After he had heard Jesus out—listening both to what Jesus was saying and to what He wasn't saying—and after he had pondered it within his own heart, the young man came to the conclusion that the requirements were too great. He walked away.

In Matthew's account, it is quietly noted that Jesus did not go after the man. There was no altering of the requirements, no compromise, no attempt to make it easier for him. He had come passionately seeking Jesus and had heard the answers of life-change empowerment for his heart and soul. But he decided that the requirements were too great, and he walked away. And Jesus let him go.

The young man left grieving because he had missed the very thing he had come seeking: rest and peace in his soul, meaning and purpose, stability and significance. He had been searching for all of that eternal "stuff" that comes with personal faith, with a clear understanding of life priorities—and how faith in God through Jesus Christ fits in. He had come anticipating life-change! He had listened. But he left empty—both in his soul and in his personhood. He left stirred but not changed.

Unfortunately, there are almost endless stories of families that wanted and needed a life-change but were not able to accomplish it, at least not in the allotted time frame. And some or all members of the families gave up and went their separate ways, whether they continued to live together or found that they could not. Generally, several challenges confront families that cannot or do not change. There are a number of reasons change does not come:

- Real change is very hard work.
- They lack commitment to the process.
- They lack honesty with self and others.
- It's easier to blame others than to take personal responsibility.
- They don't possess the necessary (often emotional) tools for success.

- They're unable to gain a healthy perspective on self, others or family as a unit.
- They're looking for a magic fix.
- Change takes longer or requires more than expected.
- The cost of change is too great.
- They lack commitment to follow up and follow through.

It may be time for a change in your family. Like the young man in the Book of Matthew, you are finding that the standard answers are not enough. He knew where he could find real insight, real answers. He came to Jesus. Your awakening may not be on your terms. Do not walk away. As you are stirred, embrace that life-change.

Follow Through with Your Desire for Life-Change

For most of us there are four key aspects to life-change. The first is to recognize the need for it. That realization can come from a deep internal desire or from an external stimulus, like being told you have to change or else you will lose something significant.

The second aspect is to make the long-term commitment to life-change. Note the issues mentioned earlier of why real life-change may not occur, and then honestly address those. It cannot remain a hope, a dream, a fantasy or something someone else can do for you.

Third, you need a life-change experience. The range of experiential opportunities is broad: class counseling or therapy, rehab, a spiritual awakening, an intense dream, an honest talk with yourself. The list goes on. Sometimes you can create the experience on your own, and sometimes it is created for you. But very often there is a unique moment of experience.

Fourth, develop a detailed plan of follow-through with steps, stages, time lines, additional experiences and celebrations. One experience alone does not produce longtime life-change patterns for most people. It requires follow-up and follow-through.

As you think of your family and the desire or need for change, identify what is needed and hoped for. Be specific. Anticipate a few key experiences to push the process on. And carefully plan follow-up opportunities to keep life-change processes going.

For Review, Reflection and Action

Key Thoughts of the Chapter

1. A common pattern of deciding to change is:
   a. Hear something, see something, feel something.
   b. Have an inner feeling of being stirred.
   c. Decide if change is "doable" at this time or not.
2. In the case study of the rich young ruler, he came seeking life-change, listened intently for answers and left without the change he sought because the cost was too great.
3. Families can miss the desired life-change for the following reasons:
   - Real change is very hard work.
   - They lack commitment to the process.
   - They lack honesty with self and others.
   - It's easier to blame others than take personal responsibility.
   - They don't possess the necessary (often emotional) tools for success.
   - They're unable to gain a healthy perspective on self, others or family as a unit.
   - They're looking for a magic fix.
   - Change takes longer or requires more than expected.
   - The cost of change is too great.
   - They lack commitment to follow up and follow through.

Questions for Further Discussion

1. Can you identify aspects of family life where it clearly would be useful to pursue a life-change? List one or two.
2. Can you identify from the above list one or two reasons why you may find completing your life-change idea frustrating?

Action Plan

Clearly identify one aspect of family life where you have successfully integrated a life-change component in the past. Celebrate it. Use it as a case study for further desired changes.

CHAPTER 5

Developing a Coaching Model That's Uniquely You

Every spring in America a tradition continues. It's called spring training. Professional athletes meet for several weeks either in Florida or the southwestern United States to prepare for the baseball season. Highly trained, well-paid athletes go back to the basics of their sport for more than a month. It doesn't matter whether you're an unknown rookie or a multimillion-dollar franchise player—everyone goes back to the basics. Run, hit and throw. Run, hit and throw. The coaching staff works to prepare the players physically, technically and mentally.

The analogy of a baseball batting coach is a great parallel of a coaching model for families. These highly paid players who hit the ball very well have an older coach who has not played for years. He becomes a partner and colleague, a friend who is a student of their game. He watches them day in and day out, studies game films, critiques the subtleties of their game style and simply gives them pointers on how to be the most effective ballplayers they can be. The coach makes a fraction of what the players earn, but the regard the ballplayers have for the coach is nearly beyond measure. The coach plays a significant role in the development of the players' potential from year to year.

When our youngest daughter was a senior in high school, she initiated a conversation with me about the power of affirmation in the life of a family. She affirmed me for my attempts at affirmation and told me how much they meant to her. Then she suggested that I read an article from *Seventeen* about how to affirm your teenage daughter. She actually had highlighted a couple of paragraphs so I wouldn't miss them.

The essence of the article was that affirmation is powerful in the life of a teenage girl. The article suggested giving less affirmation if our tendency is to give a lot, but to make it very direct and specific. I got the point. The most effective affirmation is to be pointed and concise. I went back to my daughter and said, "I think I know what you wanted me to get from this."

She smiled and said, "Dad, I love that you love me. I love that you tell me I'm amazing and all the compliments you give me. But they are very general, and if you could even give me a few less and have them be very specific, I think I would regard it more highly." She then paused, looked at me directly and said, "Dad, will you become a student of my life?"

Since the challenge before us is to develop coaching models to effectively assist our families in fulfilling the dream we share, let's now look more deeply at models that will help us in this coaching process.

High-Structure Model

The emphasis in a high-structure family coaching model is on regularity and consistency. High-structure often will refer to the discipline and instruction of the Lord. It is admirable to watch a high-structure family operate. It runs like a well-oiled machine. Timing is down pat. Expectations are clear. Everything is in its place. Everyone knows what to do, when to do it and how well it is expected to be done. It's smooth.

If you are a high-structure person, this model just makes sense to you. To you, it is how all of life should be when God is in His heaven and all is right with the universe. If you are a high-structure person, then a high-structure family coaching model creates health and happiness for you. If you are not a high-structure person, you may observe the family machinery at work and marvel that it can actually be like that. Often you feel very tired just watching it. A warning, however: Please do not impose your high-structure model on other families and refer to it as "best," "the only reasonable approach" or, God forbid, "biblical." It is but one of the useful coaching models referenced in this chapter.

For families of faith, the high-structure model will include consistent devotional times at regular intervals (daily); large amounts of biblical input, often including Bible memorization; stated benchmarks for spiritual maturity; and structured family times for serving others—the poor, elderly, shut-ins, holiday meal guests.

This model has great benefits to families. Some of the best families I know are high-structure families. The one thing often missing or less obvious, however, is nurture. And the one thing emerging lives need, whether it is a child's development or spiritual life, is nurture—a sense that things are well, that things will be fine, a sense of care and softness.

Children in particular are uniquely different from each other. We discovered that the discipline that worked so well with our two oldest children was much less effective with our third child. In fact, most of it had the complete opposite effect of what we hoped for. Coaching the two older children was relatively easy. But for our youngest son, any kind of discipline we had used before was counterproductive. He would turn it inward on himself and say, "I am really bad." His behavior got worse when we disciplined him. It was not rebellion; it was "I'm bad. There is something wrong with me."

We discovered early on that he had a multi-track mind, which we now give titles like ADD or ADHD. Before we even had terminology for it, we had to help him get on a different track. If he got on the track of "this is bad behavior," the entire situation went into a downhill spiral, and no one knew where we were going to end up. So we figured out that sometimes, instead of strong discipline and high structure with him, sitting him on our laps and talking him through the issue was far more useful. This was the beginning of the relational model of coaching for our family.

Relational Model

Highly relational people often create relational models of coaching their families. It is odd, but only a few things that motivate high-structure families actually get accomplished by relational families. A lot of things do not get done. But everyone feels fully loved and connected, both to each other and to God. You get hugged coming and going. The other models are also love-based; it's just that this one is exclusively love-based.

It's fun to watch relational model families because not just children, but everyone, gets touched, hugged, patted—endlessly and appropriately. I love to watch families who do this when they sit in church. When you are the speaker, you get to see all sorts of things happen. I often see a spouse with his arm on the back of the pew or the chair, playing with his wife's hair and rubbing her head the entire time. The receiving person can respond with either, "This annoys me. Will you quit?" or "Everything is well in the world. I feel very secure and loved."

If you operate this way in a spiritual context, people often feel loved by God as well. Sometimes the relational model is more effective at teaching people that God loves them than a high-structure or corrective model. Some of us can rub heads a lot better than we can create high structures and keep them going. So think through how you would do with a love-based, relational model.

I interviewed some families who are very verbally expressive about love. The children estimate that they were told they were loved somewhere between eight and twelve times a day, depending on what else the parents were doing. We also discovered that the children often expressed love verbally to each other. Extended family members said it to each other a lot.

A few years ago at Thanksgiving our family invited in six people from four different countries, people who didn't have anyplace to go. At the end of the day, our visitors said to Dianna and me, "We want to talk to you about your children."

We thought, *Oh, no*.

They responded, "We never have seen young adult children who seem to enjoy one another and love one another as much as yours do. How did you create this?"

Our initial response was that we didn't create it. Because our children live in different parts of the world from each other, when they are together it's nice for them. Our second response was that we were watching this and were a bit surprised ourselves; this was pretty interesting. We never knew the bonds were this strong.

They said, "Your children are more affectionate with each other than you are with them or you are with each other. We have observed you this entire day and are fascinated."

Another guest said, "We've watched you and Dianna. You like each other; you have touched a bit; and you are nice to your young-adult children, but they really seem to like each other. We want to figure out how you create this."

Our response was, "Well, send them to the ends of the earth. When they get back together for a short time (probably for three days) they will do well together. It's after the three or four days that the challenge comes." Many factors contribute to a relational, love-based model. But it involves lots of touch, affection, affirmation and verbal expressions of love.

> *Young adults say, "I grew up in a Christian home." "Then there is a pause, usually their heads go up to the side a little and they say, "But . . ." and then they do not know what to say next.*

I regularly interact with a blended family from New Jersey. The man has two daughters and his wife has one son. Plus, they have three children together. This is a unique family. It is also a rehab family, so that creates a lot of components and "stuff." But somehow they've been able to create a relational, love-based family model. When these kids are together, although the oldest ones are now in their twenties and the youngest is twelve, I have observed positive interaction at many levels and in many ways. Granted, they have all sorts of challenges, but love is what is most obvious.

Blending families is a big job, and they are far from perfect. But these people genuinely love one another, express it and honor one another, even though they are about as different as people can be.

One of them is a fashion model. One daughter is married to a physician and the other to an up-and-coming marketing guy. But there is limited competition because of this relational, love-based model.

Some of you are thinking, *You mean I can just be nice and love my family and that will work?* If you do it intentionally, yes! Families can do a lot with this model. You end up spending time together, loving each other, and out of that an intentional model of family can emerge.

Christian Lifestyle Model

This is probably the model that more families in our churches adopt than any other, though probably not intentionally. They adopt it because it's often the path of least effort and lowest structure and the easiest model to accomplish.

Expectations in these families are that you will go to the kind of college your parents went to and so on. The family displays a particular kind of life or lifestyle in which image is crucial and conformed to what is expected. This description is neither negative nor cynical in any way; it is just how the model works—with big expectations. Families say, "I don't care what your friends do. You live in this house, and in this house this is the way it is." Some children cooperate, but others challenge the expectations.

The limited focus on developing heart and soul is crucial in this model. You will find that people who've grown up in this model reach various transitions of their lives—middle school, junior high, high school, college, even young adulthood—and discover that when they think about faith and God, often their minds simply go blank. Being Christian is not something they've ever really thought about; it's just something they've always done. Personal faith can best be compared to something you simply do in your life. Much like personal hygiene, it's something you do every morning and don't think about.

Young adults who grew up in Christian homes often say, "When I think hard about God and about Jesus, I don't come up with much." If you want to know if this is a model you are accustomed to, ask yourself if you relate to the phrase, "I grew up in a Christian home . . . ."

After people say this, usually there is a pause, their heads go up to the side a little and they say, "But . . ." and then what comes next is varied. There is typically that profound "But . . ." and a significant pause. Sometimes they don't know what to say next. This is what happens if we do not intentionally develop structures and models for coaching the family.

The good part of this model, though, is that you just enjoy being Christian together. Individuals feel good about it. And we do not want to take that away from anyone, so this is a workable model. It simply has a few limitations, like heart and soul development. Faith can be reduced to personal hygiene, and expectations are common without thinking through the implications or rationale.

Covenant Model

The most significant aspect of the covenant model is that we simply represent God to each other. As we saw in the Balswick model, there is a degree of commitment, grace, empowerment and intimacy built into this model. Remember that there is always a stronger party and a weaker party, but that doesn't always remain constant. It does change in family structures. In this model there's a lot of room for grace and lots of room to put into use a wide variety of experiences.

One of the things I've tried to do over the years is to take family members with me whenever I do something significant in my faith and life. So these days when I do international travel, I give all family members, and even extended family members, my travel schedule. The practice of someone accompanying me started a long time ago when I was on the board of an inner-city mission in a tough part of Chicago. My daughter will tell you that the reason she is so passionate today as a young woman in her twenties about the needs of the urban poor is that she remembers going to the mission as a kid. Early on a Saturday morning there would be homeless people sleeping on the streets, covered up with newspaper, and she thought, *This isn't fair!*

She remembers being there with me for late-night meetings when we would serve dinners and pray with people, talk to them, sing and pray with them some more, hug them and go home. We would walk out and homeless people would be standing around a burning barrel, trying to keep warm. We would get in our minivan and go back to comfortable suburbia, and she remembers thinking, *That's not fair!* She says those experiences over the years seared into her mind the determination that if she could ever do something about it, she would.

Those kinds of experiences of all sorts, some of them not even distinctively Christian, have an impact on people. It's all under the umbrella of covenant, because you represent God to each other. Remember this list? God:

- Cares.
- Listens.
- Loves.
- Understands.
- Forgives.
- Empowers.
- Is always there.

Now, add to this list your personal favorites about how God offers Himself to you. Then offer the best of who God is to each one in your family.

Under the high-structure model we noted that it was imperative to include significant amounts of nurture. In the covenant model nurture becomes crucial, from both genders. Nurture looks different in a female role than in a male role. The female role is an obvious image. From antiquity we have endless portraits, statues, paintings and drawings of one of the greatest images from human history: a mother nursing an infant. Or you will find a child sitting on a mother's lap. You find great images in Scripture of the feminine or nurturing traits of God. We even hear Jesus saying He wants to gather lost people to Himself like a mother hen gathers her chicks. In the covenant model not just the soft side of nurture can be offered, but strength can be offered as well.

Much of what I've done over the years has been helping men deal with intimacy in their families. In a book by Frank Pittman called *Man Enough*, the author writes what I've been saying for the last twenty years: Men cannot learn intimacy from women. Men have to learn intimacy from other men. If men learn intimacy from women, even women don't like it. It's too soft. Women want men who know intimacy, but with strength. If men don't learn intimacy from other men, they either do not learn intimacy or they learn a soft version of it. This is a key reason I've committed much of my life to mentoring men. It's often the clearest opportunity men have to build intimacy and nurture into their lives.

Probably of the five family coaching models, the covenant model requires the most work. And it may be the most challenging model for men to incorporate. Parents have limited amounts of control in this one. It requires a lot more modeling, a lot more listening, a lot more personal prayer for your family. You give away power, authority and control instead of demanding it. But imagine your family for just a minute if you could really represent God to one another and give away the grace, peace and empowerment of God to them. You would have a different family.

Integrative Structures Model

Integrative frameworks are very intentional and experiential. Learning life and faith is not about learning content, not about Christian stuff, not about looking, acting or smelling Christian. It's about taking all of life and all of faith and putting it together to create some simple structures of how to make it work day-by-day and week-by-week. It is about how to make it work on Monday afternoons and Thursday mornings and throughout the week. Religious or Christian stuff works well when we are thinking Christianly; but when we are not thinking Christianly, it doesn't work all that well, for instance on athletic fields or hockey rinks. You can, however, do integrative frameworks in all of life's environments, not simply in religious settings, if the model is intentional.

Integrative frameworks also are outcome-based. Remember the questions we started with? Decide what kind of family you want. The integrative model works when people say, "This is the kind of family I'm hoping for. I'm going to create my own structures for this." The emphasis is simply on living out a practical faith. For those of you who are experiential, fun people, this is your model. What you'll discover is that you will give to the people nearest you in your family—whether it's children, siblings, extended family members—somewhere between three and twelve significant times with them in a year. In all likelihood you will impart something of God in each one of those times, and they'll remember it.

Our family discovered a long time ago that no matter how we tried, we couldn't do regular family devotionals. Even when we had them, it didn't work well. We decided that if we wanted to make family devotional times memorable, we would have to do them less often and turn them into big events. So we did Jonah and the giant fish. We went to the back of the grocery store and found cardboard and cut out a big fish. Then somebody got to be Jonah, and somebody got to be the big fish that devoured him. You only do a few of these events in a year—two to ten, maybe twenty—but they become memorable.

How do you live out your values when you drive down the road, when you walk by the way, when you're out on fishing trips and play days? The conversations and structures revolve around day-to-day concepts. For instance, you decide how much permission you give family members to make poor decisions and then learn from them. You make decisions within the structured guidelines, but with communication and coaching from within the family.

Integrative frameworks are about regular conversations and real-life examples. One of the conversations that always needs to happen with kids is the classic sex talk. Exactly when you have it depends on where you live and how much exposure your children have to community people. If the children go to public schools, then you may need to have it sooner. I've heard so many fun stories from kids who are now teenagers. They report, "My parents were so nervous. They brought it up, and I said, 'What do you want me to tell you, Dad? Are you asking me, or are you going to tell me something?'"

I actually had a teenager tell me, "My dad gave me a sex talk without mentioning the word *sex*. There were many long pauses and stutters in this one-sided conversation."

I've been coaching dads to bring up sex as if it's a normal part of life. Say, "Can we talk about the last month, son? How big an issue has porn been for you in the last month?"

So maybe the son asks, "How do you gauge how big an issue it is?"

Dad says, "Is it something you thought about once or twice or much more? When you've been with your buddies, is it something you've looked at once? Have you thought about it twice, but done nothing about it? Or have you found yourself several times a week saying, 'Man, I wish I could get some of that stuff'? That's part of the gauge, so how are you doing? . . . Not that big of a deal? Good. Can I ask you in a couple months?"

"Sure."

Now that's a very different conversation than, "Son, I need to talk to you about p-p-p-pornography. You know it's out there and you know it's this . . ." That's where the father is the authority who is saying to the younger one, "This is it, this is bad! Run!" Talk about it like this: It's out there, so what are you going to do with it?

This is true of all those sorts of issues. Maybe you are wondering about eating disorders and your daughter. Instead of immediately having some sort of intervention in which she feels like all the pressure is on her, just ask questions about her friends. Or point out someone and say, "When you see somebody like that, do you wonder if she has an eating disorder?" or "When you see somebody like that, what's the first thing that comes to your mind?"

I had that conversation with my daughter once over pizza. She had lost a lot of weight, and she went with me to get pizza for lunch. There were two girls in the booth behind us who were eating large amounts. These girls were not that big, and I said to my daughter, "I can't believe it; they must be on seven or eight plates each."

My daughter said, "You watch. If you have time, let's sit here. I promise you they will go to the bathroom and be gone ten to fifteen minutes and then come back."

"Are you serious?"

She said, "You watch. I promise you they're bulimic."

I took the time. We sat there and talked. They left and came back fourteen minutes later. I said to her, "Is that ever an issue for you?"

She paused. "No, I just needed to lose weight and wanted to, and I have lost enough."

"May I ask again?"

"Sure."

Those are normative conversations. You have them at a pizza place while you're eating and observing someone else's behavior. Those are integrative frameworks. You don't create crises. You don't create events to talk about big stuff. You have more day-to-day sorts of conversations, often regularly, about real stuff, big stuff, small stuff . . . all about life, love, faith.

For Review, Reflection and Action

Key Thoughts of the Chapter

Five models of coaching your family are presented:

1. **High-structure model**—creates a pattern of regularity and consistency in all aspects of life.
2. **Relational model**—a less structured model where family members feel very loved.
3. **Christian lifestyle model**—with the limited intentionality of this model, a family simply attempts to be "Christian" together.
4. **Covenant model**—the family represents God to one another.
5. **Integrative structures model**—an intentional and experiential model where the family seeks to live out real-world faith daily, incorporating conversations and aspects that others tend to avoid.

Questions for Further Discussion

1. As you read through the five coaching models of family, which best fits you? Describe why. What are any potential pitfalls or weaknesses of this model for you?
2. As you observe the integrative structures model, what are some normative developmental conversations that would be helpful

in your family currently (sexuality, eating disorders, pornography, dreams, love, challenges, etc.)?

Action Plan

As you observe the covenant model, ask each member of your family to affirm two or three ways you represent God to one another well within your family and two or three ways you could improve on representing God to each other.

CHAPTER 6

Dealing with the Hard Side: Family Myths, Family Lies, Family Secrets

If we're going to talk about ridding our lives of difficult family issues, we have to talk about what the issues are, how to break them and how to put the past in the past. Usually, the issue seems to be that there is a root of deception. Go through your Bible sometime and look at the four or five phrases that have *root* in them: root of bitterness, root of deception and so on. Just as there are generational blessings, there are also generational curses.

What's in a Name?

There is something in a name, both in the name you're given and in a family name. Our oldest son's name is Bo. Simply Bo. For years people have said to us, "Why do you call him Bo?"

Dianna would say, "Because that's his name."

My thinking was this: If my son takes after me and intellect is not necessarily his greatest strength, I would at least like him to be able to spell his name well! I wanted to give him the shortest name we could find. We couldn't find any with one letter, so we called him Bo.

As humorous as this was at the time, we now see a son who has developed well past the simplicity of his name. He is a leader among his generational peers as a thinker, speaker and minister. He says the hardest thing for him is that because his name is short and distinctive, and he's big and distinctive, everybody knows his name. When he goes places many people say, "Hey, Bo," and he says, "Hey, buddy, good to see you." It's hard for him because everybody remembers his name, but he doesn't necessarily remember anyone else's. There is a lot in a name.

There's also something about a family name that is passed on from generation to generation. I'm a Sanders, and it doesn't take much tracking to figure out the Sanders name. My great-great-grandfather was a medical doctor who came over from England to Boston. Immediately he went to Cleveland, Ohio, to set up a medical practice. He had two sons. The older son became a medical doctor, and the younger was an irresponsible gambler, drinker and womanizer. I descended from the younger son.

My great-grandfather had seven sons. The youngest two, a set of twins, were just a few months old when he abandoned his family. And my great-grandmother, who couldn't cope, died within three years. All seven sons ended up in an orphanage. Because there were too many of them, they didn't get adopted easily. My grandfather ended up on a work farm, which was much like white slavery in those days.

My grandmother was the oldest child of three, and her parents and her two younger siblings were in a horse and buggy trying to go across railroad tracks in the driving rain and didn't see the train. The train hit them and killed the parents. Some authorities came to school and picked up Grandmother and sent her straight to the orphanage. She never even got to go home and get her stuff.

My grandparents met at a work farm and decided they were in love and were going to run away together to start a new life for themselves. They had four sons and determined to create a stable family. And they did.

So what's in the Sanders name? Well, if you look back, you'll find some severe generational curses and some hardworking, well-intentioned people who didn't have very much emotional insight or strength. But some of the Sanderses wanted to make a different life and tried to do it. And now that Christ has come into the family name, His hand of blessing rests upon the family. So it's our job to keep passing on the blessings and make sure the curses have no power.

Honestly look at your family. What's in your name?

I recently talked with a family who just loved to tell the story of their grandpa, who was a fun, rascally old guy. They told about when he was in his late sixties and liked to take a nap every afternoon. But Grandpa had a lot of life left in him. He still liked to chase Grandmother around the house. I responded to the story by commenting that this funny old guy in his sixties had a libido just as strong as it was forty years ago, that old rascal. And they laughed about it.

But after a while it wasn't funny anymore. There were twelve grandsons, and eleven of the twelve had children out of wedlock or multiple affairs in their marriages. And what was supposed to have been a nice family now had men who couldn't control their sexuality. It wasn't funny anymore two generations later. I was asked to coach the family. As we began to pray, we discovered that Grandpa wasn't just frisky; there was a dark side to this. And it had been passed on. So what's in a name? Look a bit deeper and see.

Family Myths

Family myths are the introductory level of this "stuff" families pass on. Intentional myth deception in a family is passed on generationally. Note the words *intentional* and *deception*. We tell stories, and the stories grow and are twisted to make things seem better than they really were or maybe worse than they really were. It's subtle, but it grows and gets bigger. Family members know that the myth is not true, but, if you tell it long enough, the story gets more defined and it does seem true. That is what myths and legends are made of. Families tell them. If people who actually knew the family from years ago heard the story, they would look puzzled and respond, "Nobody who knew the family would have thought that." But the myth is repeated again and again.

Family myths also are unintentional partial truths that are passed on generationally. It could be the subtle little things, like how people in some families are somehow randomly singled out to be the black sheep. The stories start about someone. Individuals are assigned different values or roles. One is assigned as the smart one, or the successful one; another receives much of the blame. You find it in various families, particularly in immigrant families of about three to four generations.

Sometimes it's as subtle as the names people are given. Initially the story was intended to be humorous, but it is not funny because these names tend to stick to the person like the plague and can even place limitations upon him or her. I had a woman (thirty-two, blond, kind of cute, single) say to me,

> Give permission to honestly address the hard stuff in families. It's a part of healing the family. Family secrets, emotional and spiritual curses have to be exposed and then broken.

"It just dawned on me this year that when my brothers called me princess, that wasn't a good thing."

And I said, "What's that do to you?"

She said, "I always thought that was kind of fun. But now they call me 'the princess with a snarl' because I figured out how to play my parents for what I want. And my brothers really resent it."

It's subtle, but it starts to create something in a family that's unhealthy because you don't address it directly. You address it behind the scenes in subtle, deceptive sorts of ways.

The final myth occurs when stories, dates or statistics are intentionally enhanced or left out to make the image look better than reality. This consistently happens in families. As you move from generation to generation, people either will alter the facts or selectively leave out something.

Nine years ago when I was speaking in British Columbia, a minister was driving me to the airport Sunday evening. He quite proudly told me that he was a fourth-generation minister and that his wife had four previous generations of ministers in her family. He proudly told of the rich heritage and tradition they had. I listened for a long time and subtly affirmed him. Then I mentioned my own story and how different it was for me as a first-generation believer. How I longed for that heritage and wished I had a little of it.

I continued, "On other hand, the Sunday Dianna and I came to Christ in that little Alliance church in Ohio, twenty people were converted. Ever since, in every place we've been, we've seen a sweeping movement of the Holy Spirit in terms of conversions. It's really been fun. So what we don't have in rich tradition and family heritage, we have seen in the living ministry of the Holy Spirit in our lives, ministries and family. But I wish that I had your story."

There was a long silence, and then he said, "I've never seen the sweeping movement of the Spirit in my life, family or ministry."

I said, "Maybe it's because you talk too much about your heritage and you wear it around like a badge. If you'll probe just a little, I'm willing to bet that because of that pride there were some unhealthy things in the family as well—that the image got bigger and the people weren't allowed to be real people."

He said, "You've just described my sisters. I love to tell the story because I'm a minister. They don't love God now."

The introductory level of untruth in families is really subtle. It's the beginning of myth.

Family Lies

Family reality, especially for children, is what they've been told. As children's awareness grows, so does their confusion because what they've been *told* and what they *see* do not match. At times different people in the family are even given different information. For example, in family businesses, everybody has been told they have received the same amount of stocks. Everybody gets the same amount whenever there is a settlement. . . . No, they don't! Different amounts of money are given, preferences are given, different information is given to different people. I could have a full-time job doing mediation for Christian families with money. It's dreadful. It's almost like it's a curse on the family. Trying to pass on money you didn't work for to another generation can almost be a curse.

Sometimes family lies are simply the covering up of known truths. Often the truth is known but never talked about. Individuals then are included or excluded based on their capitulation to the untruth. A decade ago I was asked to deal with a situation involving an older man, seemingly a true gentleman, an elder statesman in his church and community. But he had a very dark side as well. He had molested a number of individuals in the community and even in his family. We had to bring it to light because one of the grandchildren, who happened to be married to one of the men I was mentoring, ended up in a psychiatric hospital.

I remember watching this closely because no one wanted to speak the unmentionable. But it was necessary. People then were included in or excluded from the family based on whether they sided with Grandfather or with what they knew was the truth. The problem took more than four years to work out, but the truth did come. When truth is revealed, opposition will grow in the case of family lies. Just keep in mind that the truth will set you free. It is imperative to stand on the side of truth.

Family Secrets

What are family secrets? Family secrets include abuses of all sorts. For example, one parent spanks his or her child too hard and leaves more marks than memories. The other parent stands in horror, saying, "We have to get a handle on that temper" and goes quietly to the child and says, "He (or she) didn't mean anything by it. It just got out of hand. It won't happen again. Please don't mention this to anyone."

We know this happens in "good families." But if we keep silent, people get hurt. Even people in church who smile so nicely on Sunday have tempers. If you cross them once in their homes, all the fury of hell comes out. As hard as this is to discuss, we cannot just be nice people who pretend things don't happen.

There are addictions of all sorts—not in your family, of course, but in others—from pornography on the Internet to a list of a hundred other kinds. Very nice people hide parts of their lives. It happens whether we call it addiction, perversion or some other name.

It is also necessary to mention incest and sexual abuse. I spoke at a conference in Canada five years ago where they had given me the assignment of talking about relationships, particularly communication within families. I started to speak and referred to the phrase in the Bible, "Do not let the sun go down while you are still angry" (Ephesians 4:26). There were obvious applications, I thought. But what would make a Canadian woman angry? I didn't know any angry Canadian women. The hundreds of Canadian women I did know were the nicest I had met anywhere in the world.

Then I immediately thought back to the first time I was asked to speak to missionaries at a conference about anger issues. I had to laugh. I thought, *Talking to missionaries about anger? That's ridiculous. Missionaries are the nicest people we know. Why would you talk to them about anger?* As I did my research I discovered missionaries have no control over their lives. They are in submission to the local church, the national Church, other missionaries, the mission itself. They have little say in their own lives, and it can cause some annoyance, frustration and anger.

Then I returned to consideration of the Canadian women in the region that I'd be speaking in. What would make them unable to release their anger? One obvious issue might be because control had been taken from them. On the Internet I looked at the studies of abuse, addiction, alcoholism and incest in that particular region. It was quite scary. I thought, *What do I do with this?*

Normally I stick close to my script when I'm speaking, but in the midst of the conference I had the overwhelming urge to say, "I want to talk to the men in the audience for just a minute. The abuse has to stop today! Before God, it must stop today!" Immediately many men looked down, and many men and women had big tears in their eyes. I knew we would have our hands full. And we did. Within two days nine men confessed. Two were taken to the police. Nearly 100 came forward, both men and women, seeking help because abuse had happened to them. That's just one small piece of Canada. It happens more than we want to admit. But it has to stop. Give permission to honestly address this in families. It's a part of healing the family.

Family secrets have to be exposed, as do emotional and spiritual curses. How do we help families do this? Recognize the truth; recognize the error. Bring it into the light. Renounce the untruth—personally and, if necessary, publicly. Repent of any part you have had. Sometimes you need mediation or intervention. And then personally and spiritually reclaim all lost ground. Do not leave the roots of deception, evil or bitterness there to stay.

Refocus on the Desired Outcome

In your quest for the family you have dreamed of, be courageous enough to deal with the hard side. Deal honestly with what is there or has not been there in the lives of family members. But be careful not to get distracted by these issues and give them more attention and power than they deserve. Otherwise, the issues, events and circumstances can and will gain control over and victimize you again. Find perspective to process the issues that may hold your family back, and then refocus on the dream.

For Review, Reflection and Action

Key Thoughts of the Chapter
1. Identify what is involved in and behind your family name.
2. Family myth involves intentional myths or deceptions—to make the family appear better than it is. Family myths can also be unintentional partial truths passed on generationally.
3. In family lies, reality is what you have been told in your family. Not everyone gets the same version of the truth.
4. Family secrets include intentional cover-ups of a wide assortment of abuses.

Questions for Reflection
1. Ask yourself if you are aware of any known deceptions in your family's history or any attempts to keep things hidden.

2. Ask: Am I courageous enough to address issues that may come up? What outside resources might be needed to adequately address these issues (pastor, counselor, psychologist, psychiatrist, spiritual director, lawyer, family mediator, etc.)?
3. Take a moment and thank God for the patterns of faith that are being developed in your family.

Action Plan
1. Prayerfully ask God to reveal any previously unknown family issues or deception that could limit your family's development.
2. Prayerfully and courageously identify any patterns of deception, myths, lies and secrets associated with your immediate and extended family. Admit them and bring them out into the light. Renounce the untruth and repent of the family's patterns.

CHAPTER 7

Praying Prayers That Make a Difference

I had just finished a leadership conference on mentoring at a Midwestern university. A woman stood in line to talk with me. I had known her and her young family in the past but had not seen her in fifteen years. What she said was brief and pointed. She simply encouraged me to keep reminding people of the power of prayer.

She has three older sons and a daughter. The sons are all ministers now and seem to be quite effective, at least by reputation. She said, "My sons are not the most gifted you'll ever find, but God seems to use them in unique and significant ways. From their first days in the crib until today, I've prayed the three brief prayers of Paul that you speak about over them and into them. I think it's part of the reason God uses my sons the way He does." And then with a grin she quickly stated, "God answers those prayers. Keep reminding families to pray for each other. It really does make a difference!"

Various surveys have asked people across the continent which one dimension of their spiritual lives needs to be strengthened or developed. Prayer has been the area most often identified. What if you were one of those people being surveyed? You might give the same answer.

It's safe to say that prayer is an area of life that is hard to assess.

How do you know if you're doing well enough in your prayer life? How do you know if your prayers are accomplishing anything? It seems that most of our conversations and the messages preached about prayer rest on one point: "Do more." This perception creates unrealistic expectations and sets up a difficult standard to reach.

Expectations About Prayer

Most Christians have adopted the expectation that they should pray a lot and that prayer should be long. I often hear people say, "I can't pray that long."

"Well, how long do you pray?" I ask.

"I don't know. But it never seems to be long enough."

The expectations for long prayers are ingrained. Deeply rooted, they lead to feelings of frustration, inadequacy and defeat. Ironically, these expectations are entirely unnecessary. Think about how short the prayers in Scripture are. They often stand in marked contrast to our expectations.

Another unrealistic expectation has resulted from preachers habitually stressing how early people of faith have awakened to pray. You've all heard it: Great prayer warriors throughout the ages got up at 4 o'clock in the morning to fight their spiritual battles. What preachers don't tell you most of the time is that these people lived long before electricity became part of everyday life. They went to bed soon after dusk. They considered rest an important part of their spiritual development, and for many of them spiritual dryness was directly related to a lack of rest. When preachers focus on early rising, they forget to mention how early those people went to bed. They didn't watch the 11 o'clock news. They didn't read the newspaper after dinner. They went to sleep.

Speakers also tend to take one or two isolated events and present them as normative. Allow me to use myself as an example. Not long ago I woke up at 5 o'clock. I had two and a half hours of great communion with God that morning. I could say that's normal, but it's not! I tend to sleep in more often than I awaken at 4 or 5 a.m. to pray. So in my sermon, if I don't tell you that I prayed that long early in the morning that one time only, I lead you think that's normative for my life. I might inadvertently give you the idea that you should do it all the time. The zeal of preachers to spur you on to love and good deeds has resulted in a disservice to you, the members of our churches.

With expectations like these before us, people in general have had serious difficulty measuring the results of our prayers. How do we do it? If we simply look at the kind of life we have, very often it would seem that our prayers are effective. The degree of their effectiveness, however, is hard to gauge. Consequently, we quantify effectiveness in terms of huge results, and again, those seldom measure up. When we look at the needs of our families and the perceived ineffectiveness of our personal prayers, it is demotivating.

Ingredients of Effective Prayer

Set aside the expectations. Don't be bound by them any longer. This is one area in which Christ longs to set you free. Take some time to read the prayers in Scripture. It's amazing how brief they often are. Notice, for example, Jesus' prayers for healing. He said things like, "Arise!" or simply, "Come out!" He gets to the point.

Prayer directly addresses things that only God can do. This is a key element of prayer. In Jesus' prayers recorded in Scripture, He doesn't spend a lot of time talking about whatever He is asking God to do. His prayers are pointed and specific. Jesus is not the only one in the New Testament to pray this way; Paul does it too. Paul doesn't use a lot of flowery language. He is fairly direct in his prayers. What we might consider to be "spiritual talk" in Paul's prayers really does have some pointedness to it.

She said, "My sons are not the most gifted you'll ever find, but God seems to use them in unique and significant ways. From their first days in the crib until today I still pray those brief prayers over them and into them. I think it's part of the reason God uses them the way He does. Keep reminding families to pray for each other. It really does make a difference!"

Prayer often deals with the realms of the spirit. The prayers recorded in Scripture get past human experience and engage the spirit world—a world we know very little about. We often ask God for strength, health and hope, but we tend to make our requests in terms of what we can do in our own strength. The prayers in Scripture, however, engage the forces of the spirit realm. That is where the battles are fought—the spiritual battles that Jesus already has won. Our job is to participate in these spiritual battles, to engage in the war through prayer on a level that addresses the realms of the spirit.

Prayer involves trusting God for the results. Results often are not measurable. They are nebulous in Scripture because in many cases they are confined to the realms of the spirit—the work that God is doing. It's often a process. Don't get caught up in trying to measure or quantify the results of your prayers. Trust those results to God.

Paul's Prayers as Models

Three of Paul's prayers are especially helpful as models. They deal with matters that go far beyond what we can do in our own strength. All of them are very brief. Added together, they come to a grand total of about eleven verses. It's clear that Paul was not interested in quantity when he prayed. Paul's are the kinds of prayers I want to be praying. They are the kind God longs to hear as people pray for each other as churches and families. These prayers make a difference.

Ephesians 3:14-19. The first prayer we'll talk about is in Ephesians. Paul writes:

> For this reason I kneel before the Father, from whom his whole family in heaven and on earth derives its name. I pray that out of his glorious riches he may strengthen you with power through his Spirit in your inner being, so that Christ may dwell in your hearts through faith. And I pray that you, being rooted and established in love, may have power, together with all the saints, to grasp how wide and long and high and deep is the love of Christ, and to know this love that surpasses knowledge—that you may be filled to the measure of all the fullness of God.

"I pray that . . . he may strengthen you with power." Paul's actual prayer begins in verse 16, and there he prays that the Christians in Ephesus will have power. Imagine what your family or church would be like if you followed a regular pattern of praying this kind of prayer for one another.

Dianna and I have experimented with prayers for our children. We have consciously focused far less on their behavior and more on the state of their souls. Paul prays some amazing things for the believers in Ephesus, and it is these kinds of substantive qualities that we wanted to see developed in our children.

As a pastor I realized that one of the weaknesses of the people under my care was their lack of familiarity with some of what our Christian culture has come to recognize as acceptable Christian "stuff." They didn't always use the "right" words for theological ideas or common church practices and would have lost for sure at a game of Bible Trivia. This apparent deficiency in peripheral things didn't bother me, however, because they were developing spiritual insight and integration. So we found the focus of Paul's prayer—spiritual power—to be of central importance.

Dianna and I noted as parents early on that both prayer and spiritual development are almost impossible to measure. How do we gauge what Paul means by "through faith"? The traditional method has been to look at how many people attend church services, how much we give in offerings and all sorts of other external things that, in themselves, are not bad. As I understand it, there are two ways to gauge this kind of faith, neither of them easy. One is the measure of your own love and passion for Christ. The other is the discernment and affirmation of the people of Christ as they recognize the presence of Christ in your life.

I learned a lot about praying for my family when I was a pastor. Many times I would go into the Wednesday night meeting and say, "Please don't feel any guilt from what I am about to say. I realize you all have been pretty busy and preoccupied this week, right?"

"Yeah," they would say. "How did you know?"

"This week I've sensed no spiritual power coming my way through prayer."

Surprised, they would ask, "How did you know that?"

I'd say, "Just tell me, have you prayed for me this week as much as usual?"

"No."

"I can tell. Don't feel guilty, but please pray."

Many families never have experienced that privilege—that joy—of having someone praying with and for them. It does make an incredible difference.

Look at the text again. Paul says, "I pray that you, being rooted and established in love, may have power, together with all the saints" (3:17-18). One of the key elements repeated throughout Paul's prayers is that he wants the believers to be people of love.

John Wesley, eighteenth-century founder of Methodism, once said that when he experienced the real, regenerational, sanctifying power of God, all he felt was perfect love for God and God's people. This is a key idea in Scripture: The love of Christ empowers us. I also have found in seeking after God that the closer I walk with Him, the more I love other believers. The more busy and preoccupied I am, the less others remind me of something favorable, and the easier it is to be irritated by them. Let Christ's love empower you.

Paul also wants his readers "to grasp how wide and long and high and deep is the love of Christ, and to know this love that surpasses knowledge" (3:18-19). Here is his crescendo: "that you may be filled to the measure of all the fullness of God"(3:19). One of the prayers Paul prays for the believers in Ephesus is that they will have in them the reflection of Christ Himself.

The Christian life was never intended to be lived alone. An approach like that comes from the American ideal of individualism. On the contrary, faith is to be lived out in community. Community is to be affirming. We are to note the presence and reality of Christ in one another.

As a professor, I get a steady stream of students who stop by my office to talk. During the course of our conversations, I say things like, "I watched you this week, and I saw the reality of Christ in you when you. . . ."

They often just stare, and then literally dozens of them have said to me, "No one has ever said anything like that to me before."

"Come on. You've been attending church for ten years, and no one has ever said anything like that to you?"

"Never!"

Something is missing! God has a dream of what families and the Church can be, but we're not cooperating. He has a dream that we will build each other up and affirm the presence and reality of Christ in one another. Faith works best when people discern God's purposes together—to know, love and care for one another. Take a risk. Let people know the spiritual growth and reality of Christ's presence you see in them. This is what Paul was praying for the people in Ephesus.

Philippians 1:9-11. Let's turn now to Paul's prayer for the believers in Philippi, which jumps out from the rest of the letter:

> This is my prayer: that your love may abound more and more in knowledge and depth of insight, so that you may be able to discern what is best and may be pure and blameless until the day of Christ, filled with the fruit of righteousness that comes through Jesus Christ— to the glory and praise of God.

Now, there's a prayer to pray for each other! Notice again that Paul wants his readers to abound in love. He also wants their love to abound with "depth of insight" (1:9). Literally, he's praying for discernment. We've touched on that too, but we will look at it again in more detail. In addition, Paul prays that they will be holy people. This is God's great dream—a holy people.

May you be "pure and blameless" (1:10). A.B. Simpson, founder of The Christian and Missionary Alliance, understood this part of God's dream. Simpson's understanding of holiness is the reason he stressed that Christ is our Sanctifier. It was so important to him that he included it as one of the foundational doctrines in what has come to be known as the Fourfold Gospel.

Paul's prayer is that his readers will be "pure and blameless." He goes even further by praying that they might be "filled with . . . righteousness that comes through Jesus Christ" (1:11). The focus is on Christ—not on your doing better. Holiness comes through your relationship with Jesus Christ so that your life will be "to the glory and praise of God" (1:11). Let Christ live out His holiness in you.

How do you measure that? The ambiguity is what makes this process difficult. If we're going to pray all these prayers for our families and other believers, how do we know if God answers? For one thing, we know by continuing to pray and love others the way the text calls us to love. We see God answering when we observe other believers, not with a measuring stick, but with lots of grace. We see God answering when we affirm people and say things like, "I see Christ in these ways. . . . I love you in these ways. . . . I see the reality of Christ flowing out of you when you. . . ."

How do you gauge progress? You don't. Instead, you expect and affirm progress in one another. Treat one another the same way you want God to treat you—in that acceptable, affirming, nurturing way. Make that your attitude toward each other as you pray for one another. Think about the things you so appreciate about God, and pray that they might become a reality in your family.

Let's return to this matter of insight and spiritual discernment. In the Church we've so reduced faith to our own strength that we are no longer highly discerning. We don't even know what discernment means. As I talk about discernment in churches, people say, "I don't think I've ever heard about this." That's because few people talk about spiritual discernment. Instead we rely on our measuring stick of external behaviors, how we should do better and do more. The key to identifying true development and holiness in each other, however, is to have spiritual insight.

During the summer between my junior and senior years at college, I was convinced that God was doing things in my life, gifting me in particular ways. However, in one three-week period I had four people tell me I was the most uncaring person they'd ever met. That didn't bother me because I thought God was grooming me to be a prophet. Everyone knows prophets don't have to be nice; they just set the record straight. So when people pointed out my lack of compassion, I took that as a good sign. I was much better at kicking people's backsides than nurturing their souls.

Even so, the more I thought about the comments about me being uncaring, the more it rang true that Christ wasn't that way. He was known for compassion, as well as strength. I realized I needed to explore this further. So I blocked off a three-day period and went away into the woods where there's a waterfall about 190 feet high. In that beautiful place, I sat on the hillside on a rock for three days with my Bible, my notebook and a hymnal—fasting and praying.

At the end of those three days, I said, "OK, Lord, I want to see people the way you see them." The heavens did not open up; there was no voice thundering words of affirmation; nothing spectacular happened—but a quiet sense came. I gathered up everything and left, knowing I was going to be different.

When I asked God to let me be like Christ and see people the way He did, I thought that meant seeing them with compassion. It took only a few hours, however, for me to realize that I had been given something else—the gift of discernment. That experience has been foundational to how I've lived out my faith in ministry ever since.

To see things that aren't revealed in any way other than by the Spirit—that's discernment. Paul prayed that such would be the experience of the people in Philippi. He longed for them to be able to see things far beyond what they had ever sensed before. Can we start praying that for each other? When we exercise discernment and follow the Spirit's leading in our lives, operating in God's power, we tend to be less critical and far more insightful.

Colossians 1:9-12. This is the final prayer of Paul we'll look at:

> Since the day we heard about you, we have not stopped praying for you and asking God to fill you with the knowledge of his will through all spiritual wisdom and understanding. And we pray this in order that you may live a life worthy of the Lord and may please him in every way: bearing fruit in every good work, growing in the knowledge of God, being strengthened with all power according to his glorious might so that you may have great endurance and patience, and joyfully giving thanks to the Father.

"We have not stopped praying for you." That's a great phrase! Consider the different elements of this prayer: that the believers will have the knowledge of God's will; that they will have spiritual wisdom and discernment; that they literally will walk like Christ. Those are big requests. Then Paul tops it off with his desire that God will strengthen the believers with all power. That idea is in all of these prayers.

Paul prays that God's people will know what to do with their spiritual blessings. The people are to know God's will, live a life that pleases God and bear fruit. Those are the expectations of an effective Christian life. But, again, please note the absence of time-honored phrases like "Pray harder," "Be better," and "Do more." Rather, the prayer is for strengthening with God's power so they may have great endurance and patience.

A few summers ago our family traveled several thousand miles across North America as I spoke at conferences and family camps. The majority of these folks had a theology of sanctification with an emphasis on holiness. That summer I kept track of several hundred conversations about people's understandings and experiences with the work of the Holy Spirit.

Among the numerous questions I asked them, the answers to one in particular were striking to me: "When you ask for the fullness of God's presence through the Holy Spirit in your life, do you also ask for the Spirit's power?" I only met a handful of people who said yes. I pointed out to the others that Acts talks about receiving the Holy Spirit and power. Why was that not a part of what they sought? The responses of the vast majority were varied. One group said, "I never thought about asking for power"; a second and significantly smaller group said, "I guess I assumed the Holy Spirit and power"; a third group either was confused or distrustful as to why I was inquiring about spiritual power.

I summarized the details of these conversations at the end of the summer. It was striking to me that in theological circles where we embrace the sanctifying work of Jesus Christ and exhort people to lead holy lives, we haven't given them a corresponding understanding of the difference God's power makes in their lives. It seems we have reduced even the committed Christian life to what we can do in our own strength. This may be where phrases like "Do more," "Try harder" and "Be better" are rooted.

These are not Paul's prayers for the people in Colosse. Paul prays that they will know God's power and that through it they will live out a spiritual life with "great endurance and patience, and joyfully giving thanks to the Father" (1:11-12). Imagine what the Christian life could be for church people and families if we really had an under-standing of God's power and knew people were daily praying Paul's prayer over us.

Making a Difference

Notice how short, direct and pointed these three prayers are. Rather than addressing behaviors, Paul is addressing core inner issues—matters of the soul, things that only the Spirit of God can do in believers. Finally, he's asking that they be willing to let these changes happen.

Also important is that Paul is not just presenting these things to God and leaving the matter there. He's writing to the people involved and saying, "This is what I'm praying for you." As I said earlier, affirmations have to be verbalized in order to be effective. If they are not spoken, the would-be recipients are left on their own. Pray for each other the kinds of prayers that make a difference, but don't stop there. Tell one another what you are praying and how you see God's results in each other's lives.

In summary, Paul prays five key things for the various churches:

1. Power. This is basic. You can't become the person God dreams for you to be in your own strength. We're talking about God's power in your life. It's not you; it's Christ in you.

2. Wisdom, insight, knowledge, discernment. It is in keeping with God's will for you to have some sort of spiritual enlightenment beyond what you can muster on your own.

3. Holiness. God wants believers to be holy—blameless and pure. May we make a habit of approaching one another and saying, "You know, you're an awful lot like God's Son. There's a striking resem-blance."

4. Love. Paul prays that his readers will have real love for God and one another. Jesus said that love sums up God's will: Love the Lord with all your heart and all your strength, and love other people as you love yourself. How do you do that? Ask God to teach you and make that kind of love real in your life and in the lives of other believ-ers.

5. The fullness of God. Paul prays that his friends will be filled with the fullness of God. Picture that for a moment—the height and breadth and depth of the love of God. Pray for one another to be full of God.

Passing It On

The best time of my spiritual life was when I was praying regularly with three other men. It wasn't really set up as an accountability group, as such, but we prayed for one another. We phoned and faxed each other. My phone would ring, and I'd pick it up to hear one of them say, "Martin, here's the verse I'm praying for you today." I'd pick up my mail, and there would be a fax right on top. It would have three words, "Praying for you," and a verse, a quote or a thought on it.

That was absolutely the best time in all my years of faith, not so much because I was praying more than before, or that my devotions were longer, or that I witnessed to more people and led more people to Christ, or that I preached more sermons. It was because three men loved and affirmed me. They prayed for me and held me accountable—but mostly they nurtured me, encouraging me to be like Christ. It works in small groups, and it works in families.

Take some time to meet with your God. Pray a few of Paul's brief prayers. Look for opportunities to affirm the way you see God working in the lives of your family members in answer to your prayers. Like Paul, develop the habit of praying prayers that make a difference. Then your family will make a dramatic difference in the kingdom of God.

For Review, Reflection and Action

Key Thoughts of the Chapter
1. Prayer often means entering into realms of the spirit and trusting for things God alone can do.
2. The pattern in Ephesians, Philippians and Colossians is to pray for power, love, wisdom, spiritual insight, holiness and fruit.

3. When these prayers are regularly prayed into the lives of family members, God often blesses and uses them well past any human ability.

Questions for Further Discussion

1. Can you identify concrete ways God is blessing or has blessed you and your family this past year? List them.
2. Is the pattern of prayer set forth in Ephesians, Philippians and Colossians a pattern you currently pray, or is it yet to be developed? Is there any part of these prayers you need help understanding in terms of faith, trust, theology and so on?
3. Do you currently have four or five people who are praying or are willing to pray into your life the verses we looked at? If not, will you be courageous enough to seek out several people and ask them to pray with and for you? List their names.

Action Plan

Begin to pray systematically the Ephesians, Philippians and Colossians prayers into your family's lives. Pray the prayer with them. Recruit outside prayer help as needed.

CHAPTER 8

Be Sure to Pass On the Blessing

When I was in graduate school, I discovered the power of the principle of blessing. In one of my jobs, I stocked shelves in an all-night grocery store from midnight to 8:30 a.m. Then I would make my way to class very quickly, and at 9 a.m. I would start either Greek or Hebrew. It made for a tough schedule, but it was fun to see not only who shops in the middle of the night but also the kinds of people who work all night in a grocery store.

The crew chief, twenty-seven years old, was a classic party animal. He took this shift because it was the only way to keep his drinking under control after his release from a detox facility. They sent me, as the new guy, to the back to bind all the cardboard. The binder was not working properly, and with my limited technological ability I could not make it work even on the best of days.

Finally, the crew chief came to see what I was doing back there. I informed him of the machine malfunction. He came over, took a look, punched two buttons and the machine worked perfectly. I looked at him, raised my hands and said, "Bless you, my son."

I turned to walk away, and he said, "Wait a minute." He just stared at me. All of a sudden his eyes filled with tears, and he said, "No one has ever blessed me before."

It didn't seem appropriate at that point for me to tell him I was just kidding. Instead of saying, "Thank you," I had said, "Bless you."

As he turned away, I heard him muttering to himself, "I've been blessed by someone who's going to be a priest."

Over the next two weeks, he brought in his entire family to meet me—his sisters, his mother. His mother hugged and kissed me on the cheek and thanked me for blessing her son. He brought his eighty-five-year-old grandmother to meet me. I thought, *This has huge power. He's older than I am. He's a drinking party animal. I simply said, "Bless you, my son," and it made this dramatic impact on his life. Imagine. If I do this with the people closest to me and look them in the eye and touch them appropriately and say, "Bless you," there is great power in that!*

Another example of the power of blessing occurred in a course I once taught over spring break titled "Ministry to the Family." It became clear by the end of the week that, for the thirty-five students in the class, the concept of blessing had the most profound impact. Students from a dozen very different cultures, ages and backgrounds all embraced this as a key life-change principle for families and for the Church.

The Blessing in Scripture

The biblical examples of blessing are profound and well-known. In Genesis we see God's clear promise of blessing to Abraham: "I will make you into a great nation/and I will bless you;/I will make your name great,/and you will be a blessing./I will bless those who bless you,/and whoever curses you I will curse;/and all peoples on earth/will be blessed through you" (Genesis 12:2–3).

Later in Genesis, Isaac gives the blessing to his son, saying:

"May God give you of heaven's dew
and of earth's richness—
    an abundance of grain and new wine.
May nations serve you
    and peoples bow down to you.
Be lord over your brothers,
    and may the sons of your mother bow down to you.

May those who curse you be cursed
  and those who bless you be blessed." (27:28–29)

Hear the words of the prophet Zephaniah as he offers a blessing to Jerusalem: "The LORD your God is with you,/ he is mighty to save./ He will take great delight in you,/ he will quiet you with his love,/ he will rejoice over you with singing" (3:17).

Finally, heed the words of Peter as he instructs the Church:

Finally, all of you, live in harmony with one another; be sympathetic, love as brothers, be compassionate and humble. Do not repay evil with evil or insult with insult, but with blessing, because to this you were called so that you may inherit a blessing. (1 Peter 3:8-9)

In these brief passages we see a blessing offered in at least four different settings: God to an individual, a parent to a child, prophet/leader to a city or group of people and New Testament writer to the Church.

The Blessing as Empowerment

A blessing provides impetus, security, desire, value and much more. It is beneficial in families, institutions, organizations and churches. It empowers people. It is subtle, but its power is dramatic. It says to someone:

- You are valuable.
- You matter.
- I care.
- I want the best for you.
- You can do something or be someone useful.

I was the weekend speaker in a church not long ago. I spent Friday evening through Saturday afternoon in planning meetings with the church leadership. After the Sunday morning service, I stopped the pastor's wife and said to her, "All weekend I have watched the masterful way you deal with people, listening intently, touching appropriately and saying the right word to the right person at the right time. I thank God for you and your ministry to this church."

She quietly stared and then replied, "I don't know how to respond."

I said, "You don't have to say anything. I just wanted you to know. Bless you."

Within minutes she came back and stood beside me while I concluded a conversation. As I turned to her she said, "We have served this church for fourteen years. No one has ever said anything like that to me."

I suddenly thought to myself, *Fourteen years of faithful, productive ministry in one place, and no one mentioned a word of verbal affirmation or blessing.* Fourteen years! She received a word of blessing and empowerment that day that truly made a difference.

The power of the spoken word is a key theme in Scripture. James's honesty concerning the power of the tongue makes us all quite nervous. Single words spoken can bring empowerment and blessing or destruction and curse. Those words come from our hearts and our voices. Each one of us possesses great power over other people to bless them or to destroy them.

> Instead of saying, "Thank you," I had said, "Bless you." As he turned away, I heard him muttering to himself, "I've been blessed by someone who's going to be a priest." Over the next two weeks, he brought his entire family in to meet me, the man who had blessed him!

Barriers to the Blessing

In many families and groups we build our lives on a performance mentality where people's value rests on how well they measure up to the expected standard. For some, nothing short of perfection is acceptable.

Another barrier to passing on words of blessing is our fast-paced society. Everyone is busy; everyone is tired; everyone is preoccupied; the amount of personal, quality time is limited.

A third barrier comes from a general inability to express deeply personal feelings. In some families these simply are not shared. A common response says, "They know how I feel."

A fourth barrier I will mention is that very often blessing has not been modeled in previous generations. Therefore, an individual simply does not know how, or it feels awkward, or there is a question of how it will be received. Please, for the sake of the next generation, risk it. Put on those words of blessing.

Models of Blessing

In their book, *The Blessing*, Gary Smalley and John Trent outline five elements of the blessing in Scripture:

1. Meaningful touch.
2. Always verbalized—a spoken message.
3. Attaches high value.
4. Picture of a special future.
5. Tailored to each person you want to bless.

These characteristics transcend time and cultures. They are just as effective and meaningful in North America in the twenty-first century as they were two millennia before Christ in the Near East.

The most common pattern of blessing is passed from parent to child. The blessing contains a number of forms: a direct look, a meaningful touch, a warm embrace. It is verbalized in phrases like:

- "I love you."
- "I'm proud of you."
- "Nothing you do will ever separate us."
- "God can really use you."
- "Your special ability is truly a blessing to others and to God."
- "I thank God often that He gave you to me/us."
- "You mean so much to me."
- "Your life will make such a difference."
- "I believe in you."

The blessing can come from other family members as well:

Grandparents can pass on great blessing to their grandchildren and great-grandchildren. Aunts and uncles may also speak words of blessing that can empower the next generation of family members.

The power of the blessing also can be seen in the church, coming through the words of a pastor, an elder, a church leader or any other perceptive and caring Christian. Many people serving the Lord faithfully today never have received those necessary words of blessing at home, but through God's people they find the meaning, purpose and empowerment they need to live with satisfying purpose.

Offering the Blessing

In a world that passes out far more criticism and harshness than encouragement and blessing, individual Christians and the Church find themselves in a strategic position, representing the grace of Almighty God.

Take a moment and picture the next generation around you. The next generation of:

- Your family.
- Missionaries.
- Pastors.
- Church leaders.
- Children in your community.

Now, picture them receiving the words of blessing that bring purpose, hope, courage and empowerment. You have a great part in the future of your family and the Church.

A father recently recounted a story of being on a tour of the Holy Land. As the group arrived at Mt. Carmel, there stood a towering image of Elijah, the mighty warrior of God. On the grounds nearby was a small chapel dedicated to prayer and reflection. After everyone else in the group had left the chapel, the father entered alone and for twenty minutes prayed for his oldest son, who then was in his twenties. The father asked God to use his son in mighty ways and to give him great courage. He even prayed for the same spirit of Elijah to rest upon this young man to be a warrior in the kingdom of God. The prayer time concluded, just in time for the father to board the bus with the rest of the group. He took a moment to purchase a few post-cards of the statue as a reminder of those special moments.

Later in the day he began to reflect upon what had happened in the chapel at Mt. Carmel. The experience became even more pro-found. He decided that rather than simply keeping this to himself, he would recount part of it to his son on a postcard and tell him of the prayer in particular. He carefully explained that this was not an imposition of his will, nor was it intended to put pressure on him, but was simply meant to be words of blessing.

The card gave them an opportunity to talk and pray together at new levels. Those words, spoken in prayer and expressed in writing, were empowering to the son. In the years since, that young man's character and faith have developed dramatically, and he regularly sees people give their lives to Christ.

Covenant today to intentionally influence the next generation in two ways. First, model a vibrant faith; real faith is infectious. Much of the Christian faith is better caught than taught. Second, empower and bless those around you in purposeful ways by the words you speak.

Three years ago, between Thanksgiving and Christmas, all four kids—without the others knowing about it—wrote letters or took their mom out for a meal and talked about her influence in their lives. They all said something very similar: The kind of person I am now is mostly because of the influence of my mom in my life. They did not say the same thing to me, although I know they apppreciate me sig-nificantly. But there is something about the way in which she has rep-resented God to them that clearly reminds them of the Father's love.

And now, may I offer you this blessing: "The LORD bless you/and keep you;/the LORD make his face shine upon you/and be gracious to you;/the LORD turn his face toward you/and give you peace" (Numbers 6:24–26).

For Review, Reflection and Action

Key Thoughts of the Chapter

1. A blessing gives people a sense of personal value and empowerment so they can move forward to become all God intends them
   to be.
2. There are five components to a blessing in Scripture:
   a. Meaningful touch.
   b. A verbalized message.
   c. Attaching a high value.
   d. Picture of a special future.
   e. Tailored personally to you.
3. Barriers to the blessing include:
   a. Performance mentality.
   b. Perfectionism.
   c. Limited time.
   d. Inability to express feelings.
   e. Lack of modeling.

Questions for Further Discussion

1. Can you think of people who have passed on a blessing to you?
   What did it sound like?
2. Can you identify any barriers to passing on blessings in your
   life and in your family? How will you overcome these barriers?
3. At this time, which member of your family needs to have a
   blessing spoken to him or her most? How will this person
   receive it best: written, spoken in person or put on tape? If it is
   to be spoken, should it be done privately, or would it be best to
   include others in the experience?

Action Plan

Begin to become a student of each other's lives and needs. Make
two lists—one of ways you can empower and bless each member of
your family individually and one of ways you can do it collectively.

CHAPTER 9

Getting Started:
Developing an Approach
Unique to Your Family

Families are unique, the source of endless challenges and even more joy and fulfillment. The approach of this book has not been exposition of the academic research of a professor or therapist, but observations and insights of a reflective practitioner who annually interacts in the lives of about 2,000 leaders and their families. Now here are some final reflective thoughts about the process of coaching your family.

Plan—But Be Sure to Start

There is great power in creating a clear roadmap to follow with your family. Detailed planning has great merit, both for the highly structured and for those who struggle to be decisive or cannot seem to follow through. But too much planning can bring paralysis to the direction and the relationship of the family. So plan . . . but then get started. There's a lot at stake; people's lives are moving forward.

In your plan be sure to include several things:

1. *Start simple.* It's neither necessary nor recommended to begin with a "master plan." Begin with a few items that are interesting, enjoyable and doable. Then build on your successes and create some momentum. Start with brief prayers two or three times a week. Quickly add one a week, along with a time of direct affirmation.

2. *Consistency counts.* It's better to begin smaller, establish a few good patterns and stick to the plan than to start with an ideal, lose momentum and quickly lose hope. Two small attempts a week for three months is better than a few weeks of an ideal plan that doesn't continue for very long.

3. *Start with low expectations.* Then be surprised when it goes really well. Celebrate your successes! Life-change, especially real life-change, typically comes hard and slowly, but it's worth it in the end.

4. *Consider periodic events.* Many of us will think the plan has to begin with daily routines. No, daily routines will come, but at first consider situations twice weekly (praying together); once a week (mealtime with direct affirmation and listening to one another); once a month (a family "fun" interaction); once a month (doing something special that one member of the family enjoys); every other month (a family council with simple structures). You create the next idea. . . .

5. *Plan to fail at least once (or more).* Family relationships and perfectionism do not go hand in hand for most families. One parent may disagree with this statement, but try interviewing the children and the spouse. Simply give yourselves permission not to be amazing in the beginning stages. If it takes one or more false starts, that's OK. Keep going!

Establish Your Approach—
Is That Your Final Answer?

We have asked a series of reflective questions to assist in determining your family's direction and outcomes. Take a moment to clarify your thoughts one more time. Ask the key diagnostic questions:

1. What kind of family do we want?
2. What kinds of families have we seen?
3. What kind of model best suits us?
4. What do we do with all the leftover stuff?
5. Where do we start?

Determine your best approach to develop the family you've always wanted. Which model or models will best guide your family in achieving your desired outcome? Realize that different people will reach their goals differently.

Although we've agreed on many aspects of life with our children, Dianna and I have taken very different personal approaches. We are different people in temperament and in style. As our children have gotten older, they have expressed more appreciation for their mother than they have for me. This has perplexed and annoyed me a bit, because in my thinking I've been a better father than she is a mother. But as the children have reached young adulthood, I've begun to share their perception and appreciation of their mom and to understand why for so long I didn't understand her approach.

Both in my mind and in reality I've tried really hard to be a good dad. I worked at it. I read books on it. I prayed about it. I experimented with it. I made lists of things to do and not to do. Dianna, on the other hand, just did what she did naturally and instinctively. She didn't seem to work as hard at it. By temperament she is calm; she doesn't react; she doesn't raise her voice. She decided early on not to speak negative things nor say anything in negative ways. So from the kids' perspective, she not only was an ideal mom, but in their minds the best mom ever, because her responses always seemed appropriate.

From my perspective she could and should have said more, done more or done what she did with more flair. From the kids' perspective it was the security of her appropriateness and consistency that they could count on. And as the kids have gotten older they have shown such appreciation for that in their own lives and have expressed thanks to her. She had an established approach, just as I had mine.

Empower

In the initial planning and over the years, be sure to include family members in the planning and evaluation process. After all, it's their lives and family too. The coaching process of family development does not allow much room for imposing edicts on other family members. Rather, it is the relational living out of a common purpose that makes empowerment happen.

Our family spent nine years living in the Chicago area. Dianna and I had a dream of having a cabin on a lake in the woods of Wisconsin. Because of additional graduate school and other issues, the dream never became reality. Our summers often were spent traveling to conferences, camps and visiting family several states away. As our children got older and felt more free to express their opinions, they unanimously told us how happy they were that we never got that cabin in the woods.

We were surprised to hear their perspective. They believed that the cabin would have been a relaxing but one-dimensional experience. They realized they had been able to visit half the states in America in five years, meet lots of people, have many unique experiences, get away with a few things while parents weren't around and create lots of memories as a family. Together they voiced how happy they were that we parents never got our dream of a summer getaway.

Rather than discovering family members' opinions too late, as much as possible include everyone's input throughout the stages of life and development. Give each member permission to express his or her own particular preferences. Help one another reach your dreams.

Give Yourself Grace

Remember, your plan for family coaching is not the law but a goal. It's a guideline, which of necessity implies that it is flexible. All families will fail to reach their ideals at some point. That's OK. Give yourself and one another some grace. Families typically fail by missing the balance between being too rigid and too lenient, between no grace and too much grace. Give yourself and one another permission to fail once in a while.

Just as the Christian faith is a religion of second chances, family life can offer second chances as well. Think about it. We all have seen difficult-to-raise children who have turned out to be good parents. How many people do you know who were not good parents but have become very good grandparents? And you may even know people who were not good kids or good parents or even good grandparents, but who, because of age, wisdom or life-change are becoming very good great-grandparents! Give yourself some grace. God does!

Build Flexibility into Your Coaching Plan

It's challenging to know when to flex, when to make the current instance an exception to the plan and when yet another exception will simply nullify the whole idea of even having a plan. It's a balancing act. You will not know if you made the best choice until sometime later. So once again, offer yourself and one another some grace if you can.

Start with low expectations— then be surprised when it goes really well! Celebrate your successes! Life-change, especially real life-change—typically comes hard and slowly, but it's worth it in the end.

One of our sons had the hardest time growing up of all of our four children. He seemed to need a little extra attention and care and usually saw the world differently. For a time we had the principal's office at the high school on speed dial because we seemed to need to interact with him so often. We received a call one day from the high school. The principal said, "We have a concern about your son." It was Career Day in his freshman year, and our son had announced that he wanted to be dictator of the world. "Normally we would laugh it off," offered the principal, "but because of some of his other behavior issues, it causes us considerable concern. And we just needed you to know about this and have you interact with him to see if he was just having fun and playing with us. Let's find out what's behind it."

So we decided to enter this conversation rather casually and try not to react. We said, "What's behind that?"

Our son said, "I seriously think I'd be a good dictator. Many places in the world need a good dictator, and I think I'd be good at it."

I paused for a moment, thinking how to respond rather than react, since my first instinct usually is to react—particularly in more aggressive than understanding ways. Finally I said, "Have you ever studied effective dictators?"

He responded that he had not.

And I said, "Well, typically dictators gain those positions in one of three ways. First, you get into a power position in whatever way you can and take control of people's lives, often with harshness. The second way is that you and your group take over the existing government with a military coup. This typically requires a great deal of bloodshed and heartache for the nation. The third way you become a dictator is by gaining the respect and trust of the people so that they realize it's actually a good thing for you to have control of the nation and their lives. And even though they wish for freedom, it's a good kind of existence, living in the shadow of your power and control."

Immediately our son said that the last one was the kind of leader he'd want to be.

"OK, then if you're going to be that kind of dictator-leader," I said, "you need to know that leaders are readers, so you need to read up on leadership." And so at fourteen years old he began to read a list of books I gave him. The first one was *Leadership Secrets of Attila the Hun*. Also in the top five on the list was *Victory Secrets of Attila the Hun*.

What transpired in the next year was fascinating to all of us. He read everything he could get his hands on from leaders around the world, from Mao Tse-tung's "little red book" to biographies of American presidents. He read dozens and dozens of books. About fourteen months after our initial conversation, one night at dinner he declared that he was no longer going to become dictator of the world. When we inquired as to what had changed his mind, he said, "I don't think I would be kind enough to the people. They would need someone kinder."

A number of things happened in his life because we reflected and responded rather than reacting. First, an unrealistic and inappropriate response or remark turned into a developmental coaching time. Second, he worked through issues of his own life to figure out what he was like and how to develop beyond that. Third, it became an educational time for him to read and reflect and come to grips with bigger issues of the world around him. And last, he felt he was validated as a person rather than being chastised as a child.

I wish I could tell you we always responded this well, but this one time sticks in my mind. We used an effective approach to what otherwise could have been a family argument and a potentially embarrassing situation.

As you create and adjust your plan over time, be willing to mix and match models and approaches. Our family has used all five models with differing levels of effectiveness. Don't rigidly embrace one. Everyone in the family is not the same type of person. As the family matures, develops and changes, it's often beneficial to adjust the approach and model as well.

Discover the Power of Small Choices

As with so many things in life, the difference in outcomes in your family will be affected more by the subtle, small stuff than the monumental choices.

American Thanksgiving is a significant time for families. The four-day weekend is the busiest travel weekend of the year across the United States. How a family decides to spend Thanksgiving Day together influences so much in the family. Some families gather the entire extended family, the whole clan, in one place. They celebrate family and their personal blessings of the year, often thanking God for His blessing. It's a great time to be family. However, the blessing often is kept within the family; it isn't shared.

Other families will invite in friends, most often people who are like them in many ways. The family flexes to include others from outside to share this special time together. This spreads the influence of the family blessing, but the angle of influence is still somewhat narrow.

Still other families use this national holiday as a day to serve others. The family takes on a project to go and help with meals for those who have significant life challenges. The early part of the day is spent cooking, preparing and serving meals and bringing a bit of hope to those who need some extra care at this time of life. Typically, the family then gathers at home to have their own holiday meal and enjoy "just their family." Together they have served, ministered, helped, encouraged, offered hope. The family feels good about the experience. It's a great way to spend this important family holiday. There is one issue, however. The family went out to serve and then came home to enjoy their blessing privately.

The final family model of Thanksgiving is somewhat different. This approach sees the family, often operating within a covenant context, as bringing others under its personal umbrella of blessing and grace. The family invites outsiders, often previously unknown to the family, to share the unique day in their home and to be a part of their family.

One family I know of invited a man in his late twenties who was down on his luck to come and join their Thanksgiving meal. This man worked at a group home for developmentally disabled adults. The schedule changed at the last minute, and he was called to work. Only one resident, a man with Down's syndrome, was left in the group home that weekend. So the young man asked if he could bring the resident along. Later he discovered that one of his colleagues, a single mother with a biracial baby, was not invited to be with her family due to tensions over the birth of the baby and issues surrounding the baby's father. Still later, there was one more request to include another "holiday orphan" with challenging life circumstances.

After a brief family meeting and some explanation of safety issues within the family, it was agreed to invite this unique group of people into their home. The experience was so positive that it became a tradition to bring in outsiders whose life experiences were quite unlike their own, to expand the family covenant to include a wide range of people. Over the years this family tradition has been a blessing to many "orphans."

If a decision about one day can make that much difference in a family, don't rule out the power of a multitude of small, subtle choices.

Go ahead. Get started. Make a family. Pass on the blessing for generations.

Here is a blessing for your family that I would like to leave with you:

May you develop the family you've always wanted.
May God give you the strength;
May God give you the courage;
May God give you the wisdom;
May God give you the discipline;
May God give you the love to make it work.
May your fantasy turn into a dream,
and may your dream turn into reality for your family.
May you discern the difference between annoying things to ignore
and destructive things that need to be addressed.
May you give each other permission and grace in the process.
May you speak words of affirmation,
encouragement and love to each other.
May God give you the family of your dreams.
May it be enjoyed for generations to come in your family.
God bless you!

For Review, Reflection and Action

Key Thoughts of the Chapter

1. Establish a personal approach to coaching your family. Ask those five diagnostic and reflective questions again:
   a. What kind of family do we want?
   b. What kinds of families have we seen?
   c. What kind of model best suits us?
   d. What do we do with all the leftover stuff?
   e. Where do we start?
2. In the development of your family's plan, be sure to remember:
   a. Start simple.
   b. Consistency counts.
   c. Start with low expectations.
   d. Consider periodic events.
   e. Plan to fail at least once (or more).
3. Remember to give yourself grace. The Christian faith is a religion of second chances.
4. Discover the power of small choices, like how your family spends Thanksgiving Day.

Questions for Further Discussion

1. Identify two of the five core questions to focus on first, and decide how you plan to address them soon.
2. In terms of failure, most families either give themselves too much grace or not enough. If one of these is your pattern, how do you plan to address it?
3. As you reflect upon the power of small choices, is it time for you to rethink Thanksgiving Day? If so, how?

Action Plan

Using the five questions and the Apollo approach, create as a family a working plan to fulfill your dream of the family you have always wanted.

Bibliography

A Father's Legacy: Your Life Story in Your Own Words. Nashville: J. Countryman Books, 2000.

Arterburn, Stephen, Fred Stoeker and Mike Yorkey. *Every Woman's Desire*. Colorado Springs: Waterbrook Press, 2001.

Balswick, Jack, and Judith Balswick. *The Family*. Grand Rapids, MI: Baker Books, 1991.

Balswick, Judith, and Boni Piper. *Life Ties*. Downers Grove, IL: InterVarsity Press, 1995.

Bandler, Richard, et al. *Changing with Families: A Book about Further Education for Being Human*. Palo Alto, CA: Science and Behavior Books, 1976.

Blankenhorn, David. *Fatherless America*. New York: Basic Books, 1995.

Brown, Daniel A. *Unlock the Power of Family*. Nashville: Sparrow Press, 1994.

Canfield, Ken R. *The Heart of a Father*. Chicago: Northfield Publishing, 1996.

Chapman, Gary D. *The Five Love Languages of Teenagers*. Chicago: Northfield Publishing, 2000.

———. *Five Signs of a Functional Family*. Chicago: Northfield Publishing, 1997.

Chapman, Gary D., with Randy Southern. *The World's Easiest Guide to Family Relationships*. Chicago: Northfield Publishing, 2001.

Chapman, Gary D., and Ross Campbell. *The Five Love Languages of Children*. Chicago: Northfield Publishing, 1997.

Covey, Stephen R. *The Seven Habits of Highly Effective Families*. New York: Golden Books, 1997.

Dillow, Linda, and Lorraine Pintus. *Intimate Issues*. Colorado Springs: Waterbrook Press, 1999.

Ferguson, David, et al. *Parenting with Intimacy*. Wheaton, IL: Victor Books, 1995.

Foley, Sallie, Sally A. Kope and Dennis P. Sugrue. *Sex Matters for Women*. New York: Guilford Press, 2002.

Gangel, Kenneth O., and Jeffrey S. Gangel. *Fathering Like the Father*. Grand Rapids, MI: Baker Books, 2003.

Grunlan, Stephen A. *Marriage and the Family*. Grand Rapids, MI: Zondervan, 1984.

Guernsey, Dennis. *The Family Covenant*. Elgin, IL: David C. Cook Publishing, 1984.

Hamrin, Robert D. *Great Dads*. Colorado Springs: Cook Communications, 2002.

Hansel, Tim. *What Kids Need Most in a Dad*. Grand Rapids, MI: Fleming H. Revell, 1989.

Harley, Willard F., Jr. *His Needs, Her Needs*. Grand Rapids, MI: Fleming H. Revell, 1994.

Jakes, T.D. *Daddy Loves His Girls*. Orlando, FL: Creation House, 1996.

Joy, Donald M. *Bonding*. Waco, TX: Word, 1985.

——. *Re-Bonding*. Waco, TX: Word, 1986.

LeBey, Barbara. *Family Estrangements*. Atlanta: Longstreet Press, 2001.

Leman, Kevin. *The Birth Order Book*. New York: Dell Publishing, 1985.

——. *Bringing Up Kids Without Tearing Them Down*. Colorado Springs: Focus on the Family Publishing, 1993.

——. *Making Children Mind Without Losing Yours*. Grand Rapids, MI: Fleming H. Revell, 2000.

Maxwell, John C. *Breakthrough Parenting*. Colorado Springs: Focus on the Family Publishing, 1996.

McDowell, Josh, and Dick Day. *How to Be a Hero to Your Kids*. Dallas: Word Publishing, 1991.

McGee, Robert S. *The Search for Significance*. Houston, TX: Rapha Publishing, 1985.

McGraw, Phillip C. *Relationship Rescue*. New York: Hyperion, 2000.

McMinn, Lisa Graham. *Growing Strong Daughters*. Grand Rapids, MI: Baker Books, 2000.

Omartian, Stormie. *The Power of a Praying Parent*. Eugene, OR: Harvest House Publishers, 1995.

Payne, Leanne. *Crisis in Masculinity*. Grand Rapids, MI: Baker Books, 1995.

Pipher, Mary. *The Shelter of Each Other: Rebuilding Our Families*. New York: Ballantine Books, 1996.

Pittman, Frank S. *Man Enough: Fathers, Sons, and the Search for Masculinity*. New York: Perigee, 1994.

Rainey, Dennis. *Ministering to Twenty-First Century Families*. Nashville, TN: Word Publishing, 2001.

Smalley, Gary, and John Trent. *The Gift of the Blessing*. Rev. ed. Nashville: Thomas Nelson, 1993.

——. *The Gift of Honor*. New York: Pocket Books, 1987.

——. *The Language of Love*. Pomona, CA: Focus on the Family Publishing, 1988.